The Problem with GOD

The Problem with GOD

Why Atheists, True Believers, and Even Agnostics Must All Be Wrong

PETER J. STEINBERGER

Columbia University Press
New York

Columbia University Press
Publishers Since 1893
New York Chichester, West Sussex
cup. columbia. edu

Library of Congress Cataloging-in-Publication Data
Steinberger, Peter J., 1948–
The problem with God : why atheists, true believers, and even agnostics must all be wrong / Peter J. Steinberger.
pages cm
Includes bibliographical references and index.
ISBN 978-0-231-16354-5 (cloth : alk. paper) — ISBN 978-0-231-53520-5 (ebook)
1. God. I. Title.

BL473.S76 2013
211—dc23
2013000567

Cover Design: Mary Ann Smith

Columbia University Press books are printed on permanent and durable acid-free paper.
This book is printed on paper with recycled content.
Printed in the United States of America

c 10 9 8 7 6 5 4 3 2 1

For Mo, my goddess

CONTENTS

The Problem with GOD

I

THE PROBLEM WITH GOD

Late one night in the summer of 1969, sitting at a red light on the corner of Webster Avenue and Gun Hill Road in the Bronx, I had an epiphany.

Now traditionally an epiphany is a kind of religious experience. For example, there's something called the Feast of the Epiphany. You may have never heard of it, and if you haven't you'd hardly be alone, but in certain Catholic circles it's actually a fairly big deal. The Feast of the Epiphany celebrates the moment when the Magi—the three wise men—suddenly realize the divinity of Jesus. That was their epiphany, in Palestine. My epiphany, in the Bronx, was different. It wasn't a religious epiphany. It was the opposite. It was a rational epiphany, an epiphany of reason. But an epiphany nonetheless.

So there I am, sitting in my beat-up Plymouth Valiant, waiting for the light to change, surrounded, front seat and back, by the Archives—meaning all the old newspapers, maybe three months' worth, maybe even six, that I hadn't gotten around to throwing out. Even though it's two or three in the morning, it's still really warm. And humid, very humid. The air-conditioning isn't on, because the Valiant—it's a '63—doesn't have air-conditioning. So the windows are rolled down, all the way. But there's no breeze. And the Bronx, at least on that corner, is a ghost town. Nobody there, nobody at all. No cars. No people. Utter silence. Kind of spooky.

But then I notice that in fact I have company. On the sidewalk, across the street from the driver's side, leaning against a lamppost, there's an old guy. Just leaning there, all alone, looking at me. I look back at him. And I realize that he is—as we used to say—a bum. There's a bum on the corner at three o'clock in the morning in the Bronx, just standing there. And in fact—the Bronx being the Bronx—there's really nothing too surprising about that.

But this turns out not to be your ordinary bum. Because he looks at me, our eyes meet, he straightens up, points his finger, and intones across the roadway in a raspy voice: "Repent young man! Kneel down before God and pray!"

He has scraggly gray hair, a thick, scruffy beard, and no teeth. He looks like Gabby Hayes. Now for those of you who are a lot younger than me, Gabby Hayes was, after a fashion, a star of the silver screen. I was actually one of his fans. That's because I loved old Hopalong Cassidy movies—there were dozens of them, and as a child I watched them on television most every Sunday morning before anyone else was up, right after "The Modern Farmer"—and Gabby Hayes was Hopalong's comical sidekick. In those days, every cowboy had a comical sidekick. Gene Autry had Pat Buttram, Wild Bill Hickok had Andy Devine, and Hopalong Cassidy had Gabby Hayes—a grubby, gnarly, utterly toothless old cowpoke with sore feet, a quick scowl, and a sheepish grin, though also a tough enough customer when the chips were down. Gabby had a signature phrase: "You're darn tootin', Hoppy." That's what he would say. He said it every time he agreed with Hoppy, which was pretty much all the time. And then, after he said it, he'd munch on his gums once or twice, just for emphasis.

I remember, when I was still a little boy, seeing a photograph of Gabby Hayes in *Look* magazine, attending some kind of Beverly Hills gala. He was wearing an Italian three-piece suit, exquisitely tailored. His hair was perfectly combed, the beard was trimmed, his teeth were in, and there was a large diamond ring on his finger. A dapper fellow, indeed. Even though I was just a kid, I suddenly realized that Gabby was making good money in Hollywood. Of course he was. Probably had a nice home in Bel Air, drank martinis poolside, dined regularly at the Best Places. I think that's when I understood, really for the first time, the difference between an actor and a role. A mini-epiphany.

Anyway, there's Gabby's twin brother standing on the corner under the streetlight. Only he's not wearing a three-piece suit. He's wearing something closer to rags. "Kneel down before God and pray!" he says. "Pray for forgiveness!"

I laugh. I decide not to respond. Why would I? But then, for some reason, I change my mind. "Aw, c'mon," I call out—good naturedly—into that otherwise silent night. "God's dead. You know it and I know it." I'm twenty years old, you see, and had read Nietzsche. Well, at least I'd read a little Nietzsche.

His face immediately brightens—like some old shipwrecked guy, all alone on a desert island, who suddenly sees an ocean liner on the horizon, heading his way. "That's to you," he says, not unreasonably. And then, perhaps just a bit tentatively, "but you don't know what you're talking about."

I laugh again. "Maybe so," I say cheerfully. "But let's face it, pal, you don't know what you're talking about either."

He blinks. And then he munches on his gums.

As I drive off and make my turn—this was not the road to Bethlehem, it was the road to 238th Street and Van Cortland Avenue West—it occurs to me, rather to my surprise, that I'm actually right. Neither of us knows what the heck we're talking about. And believe it or not, I feel pretty good about that. It wasn't often in those days that I felt I was right about something, and so it feels good—even if being right meant I didn't know what I was talking about.

And then it hits me like a ton of bricks. Right there. In the Bronx. A ton of bricks. Neither of us, neither me nor the bum, knows what we're talking about because, in fact, we aren't really talking about anything at all.

I see it clearly. The world suddenly opens up. I understand. We don't know what we're talking about because neither of us is talking about a darn thing. I mean this quite literally. When we're talking about God, we're talking about nothing at all.

That was my epiphany. Might not seem like much to you, but to me it was staggering. And really, you should think about it. Because if I was right—and if I *am* right, since I haven't changed my mind—then it turns out that an awful lot of people have been barking up the wrong tree for an awfully long time.

When we're talking about God, we're talking about nothing at all. That was my epiphany. That was my thought. And ever since then—sometimes in the back of my mind, sometimes in the front—I've been trying to work it out.

And by George, I think I've got it. In fact, I know I've got it.

Human beings—*all* human beings except small children and maybe some insane people—think about the world in terms of cause and effect.

Once we understand this simple fact, we can see that the question of whether or not God exists is literally a non-question. It's a question that's not really a question at all, because it's not asking anything that makes any sense. It's simply unintelligible—and there's no interpretation, no line of thought, no intellectual strategy that could possibly make it intelligible.

I'm not saying here that the question of God's existence is an incredibly difficult one. I'm not saying it's very, very complicated, maybe too complicated for any one person. I'm not saying it's something about which people will always disagree, or that it's too bound up with our emotions to allow for clear thinking. I'm not saying that the crucial evidence is lacking and will always be lacking, or that the evidence, such as it is, will necessarily be inconclusive so that those who believe will never convince those who don't believe, and vice versa.

I'm saying something very different: it is literally, utterly, completely, entirely and eternally impossible even to conceive of what a meaningful answer would look like.

The structure of ordinary human thought—the way that the everyday human mind, yours and mine, operates and has always operated—is such that it will never, ever make any sense to say that God either does or doesn't exist. It's literally impossible for ordinary human beings at any time and in any circumstance ever to imagine the existence of God, and equally impossible for them at any time and in any circumstance ever to imagine the non-existence of God. We will never, ever be able either to entertain or to deny God's existence. These are thoughts that no ordinary human being can possibly have, because there literally are no such thoughts.

Theism, of whatever kind, must therefore be dead wrong. At the same time, atheism, however formulated, must also be dead wrong. And strangely enough, agnosticism must be wrong as well.

The argument is, in a sense, breathtakingly simple. Deep down—and sometimes not so deep down—it's an argument we all know. We don't say it out loud very often, we don't make it explicit, we don't often share it with our friends, but we know it. By the way, I'm not actually sure why we don't say it more frequently or more openly, even or especially to ourselves. Maybe it scares us. Or maybe we just don't remember it. Maybe we're distracted. After all, we're busy people. But things would be a lot better in all kinds of ways if we owned up to it—if we permitted ourselves to say out loud what we already know.

It is impossible—literally impossible—for us to imagine anything existing in the world that wasn't caused to exist by something else. Everything that you see, touch, feel—every object, without exception—is an effect of a cause or set of causes. No object could exist unless it had been brought into existence by something other than itself. Nothing appears simply and entirely out of thin air, from nowhere. The idea of something appearing out of thin air is an idea we can't have.

So for example: I wouldn't exist if my parents hadn't—well, you know what. But more, it's impossible for me to imagine my existence without my parents having done the thing that caused me to exist—or at least without something functionally similar having happened, perhaps involving test tubes and embryo cultures and other scientific stuff. After all, I'm here. Sitting right here at my computer. Writing this book. That's a fact. But the fact that I exist is a fact that needs to be explained, and the explanation has to be a cause. The explanation of my existence in the world has to be that something (or some number of things) caused me to exist. If nothing caused me to exist, I wouldn't be here. I wouldn't—couldn't—exist.

And so too for, say, the computer I'm working on. It wouldn't exist if someone hadn't made it. How could it possibly exist if it hadn't been made to exist? It couldn't. Or yet again: the rainstorm outside my window wouldn't exist—and couldn't possibly exist—without the atmospheric conditions and processes that produced it. Nothing exists, at least not according to our lights, that wasn't the result of something else. It's impossible to imagine something arising out of absolutely nothing.

Of course, things that cause other things to exist are themselves things that were caused to exist by still other things. If my parents caused me to exist, my grandparents caused them to exist; and my great-great grandparents caused *them* to exist. The tools that were used to make my computer were themselves made by other tools, which were, in turn, made by still other tools. The atmospheric conditions that created the rainstorm outside my window were the result of other, previous atmospheric conditions, which were the result of still other, previous atmospheric conditions, and so on.

In all of this, by the way, notice one important fact. For each and every case, without exception, the cause precedes the effect in time. The cause comes first, the effect comes later. Maybe only slightly later—maybe only a split-second later, maybe only a nanosecond—but later nonetheless. Has to be. That's part of what it means to be a cause and an effect. It can't be the case that I was created before the act of sex that caused me to be created. The act came first. Of course, I would guess that my parents did have sex after I was conceived—and after I was born. Probably more than once. Not, I should add, a thought that I care to dwell on. But however that may be, those subsequent acts of sex didn't cause me to exist. The one that caused me to exist occurred—had to have occurred—before I came into existence. Similarly, it can't be the case that the tools that made my computer didn't exist until after the computer came into being. How could those tools have made the computer if they didn't already exist in the first place? Or, to put the same point in a different way, how could the computer have been made if the things that made it only came into existence after the computer had already come into existence? The cause has to come first. To deny this is to be profoundly dysfunctional, indeed utterly and completely out of touch with reality.

Now all of this seems straightforward enough, but there's a problem. If everything that exists is preceded in time by something other than itself, by something that caused it to exist, then there must—absolutely must—have been something that existed before everything else, something that got the world going, some First Thing that caused the second thing and thus launched the whole process. It's impossible for us to imagine that the world didn't start. Something must have caused the world to exist. We must believe there was a beginning. We must believe that the world was caused by something other than itself. Remember, no thing comes out of nothing or from nowhere. Everything that exists was caused to exist by something else, and this applies as much to the world itself as it does to me or my computer. It's just impossible for us to think that the world sprang up from nowhere.

And why is that a problem? It's a problem because if we must believe in some First Thing that got the whole process going, then we must also believe that this First Thing existed; and if everything that exists must be caused by some previous thing other than itself, then the First Thing, like everything else, must have been caused by some previous thing other than itself—in which case the First Thing cannot have been the First Thing. We can't think otherwise. No thing springs up from nowhere, not even the First Thing. So if something caused the First Thing, then we must, absolutely must, believe that there was a Pre-First Thing—or a Really

First Thing—that caused the First Thing to exist. In which case, of course, the First Thing wasn't really the first thing at all. It was the second thing, not the first. The thing that caused it to exist must have come first. But of course, the Pre-First Thing or Really First Thing must also have existed, hence must have been caused by something prior to it—a Really, Really First Thing. And so on, ad infinitum.

Think of dominoes.

Every year around Christmas, the big—and now-defunct—department store in my old hometown would set up a long column of dominoes. Hundreds of them, maybe even a thousand, all lined up like soldiers, one right next to the other, in a twisting, looping, labyrinthine path that snaked around and through a miniature winter wonderland. Each afternoon, at the appointed hour, they'd knock them down. The whole chain reaction, from the first falling domino to the last, took about thirty seconds. At night, they'd set them up again for the next day. Pretty neat watching them fall, especially if you're, say, five.

A sad day it was, by the way, when that old store went belly-up. I don't know what caused it to go under. I know *something* caused it to go under, I'm just not sure what. That store had, among other things, the best Santa—and as you'll see, I'm actually pretty big on Santa.

In any case, there they are, the dominoes, all in a row, standing at attention, side by side, ready to be knocked over, one after the other. Now we know—assuming atmospheric conditions are right—that the very last domino will not and cannot fall until the one right next to it, the second-to-last domino, falls, knocking the very last one down. The fall of the second-to-last domino causes the very last domino to fall. And we know as well that the second-to-last domino won't fall until its neighbor, the third-to-last domino, causes it to fall. And so on. But none of this will happen—no dominoes will fall, no five-year-olds will squeal with delight—unless and until the very first domino falls. The very first domino has to start the process by falling. There has to be a beginning, otherwise no falling dominoes. And so there you have it: the first domino—we might call it the First Domino—is what causes the whole thing to happen. But no, that won't do. Because, of course, dominoes don't fall by themselves, not even the very first domino. So if the very first domino falls, then something or someone—the wind, an earthquake, my friend Vivian—must have caused it to fall. Which means that the very first domino didn't really start the process. Something or someone else did. Now let's suppose the culprit was Vivian. With the casual flick of a finger, Vivian knocked over the very first domino, which in turn knocked over the second domino, and there they go. So it's really Vivian who started the whole thing. Vivian's the cause. But then we naturally have to ask: where did Vivian come from? Because Vivian herself didn't appear out of nowhere. Something caused Vivian to exist. Of course, Vivian's pretty much like me. She came into existence—she was caused to exist—by something her parents did; and they, in turn were caused to exist by something their parents did; and so on, ad infinitum.[1]

But this "ad infinitum" stuff is no good. Because—and now let's forget about dominoes and get back to the bigger question—we have to believe that everything is caused by something else; hence we must believe that the world itself started somewhere; in other words, there must have been a beginning, an original cause among all causes, a First Thing, because nothing exists that has not been caused to exist by something else. But of course, that First Thing, since it existed, must itself have been caused by something else, hence there cannot have been a First Thing; so it's completely and entirely impossible that there wasn't a First Thing and completely and entirely impossible that there was a First Thing.

Now here's a simple fact. Either something is or is not the First Thing. It can't be both. You can't have the concept of a First Thing that is not a First Thing. There's no such idea. And if you like, we can say it the other way around as well: you can't have the idea of something that is not the First Thing but that also is the First Thing. Again, no such idea. But because we think of the world, and have to think of the world, as a matter of cause and effect, we have to believe *both* that there was a First Thing and that there was no First Thing—and there is no concept, no form of thought, no image, no idea, that can make sense of that.

Let me try this again in a slightly different way, just to hammer home the point: the logic of cause and effect—the way the ordinary human mind works—absolutely requires that we have a concept of a First Thing (the thing that started it all) which is, at the same time, not the First Thing (since something else must have caused the allegedly First Thing to exist). But there is no such concept and there cannot be any such concept. You cannot have the idea of something that is what it is and, at the same time, is not what it is. There is no idea there. It's not a thought that we can have.

So then maybe what we ought to do is simply reject the idea that there was a First Thing. Just forget about it. But no, that isn't gonna work. Because in a world of cause and effect, there *must* have been something that originally caused the world to exist, which means there must have been a First Thing. Well okay then, let's just embrace the idea that there was a First Thing. But no, in a world of cause and effect, there must have been something that caused the First Thing to come into existence, which means there could not have been a First Thing. Well, fine. If there couldn't have been a

First Thing, let's just give up on that idea. But no, we've just seen what happens there. Something must have started it all. And so on, and so on . . .

Historically, the First Thing has sometimes been called the Unmoved Mover. A fancy term for a simple point. The Unmoved Mover is a mover because it "moves" other things. That's basically another way of saying it causes other things to exist. It is itself, however, unmoved—in other words, nothing caused it to exist. So it came first. It was the First Thing. And, of course, another word for this is God. The argument for God, then, goes roughly as follows.[2] Since the world exists, something must have started the world. Something must have caused it. But this something cannot itself have been caused by something else, otherwise it wouldn't have been the cause of everything. Something else would have preceded it, hence something else would have been the cause of everything. So we have to rule that out; and this means that we have to conclude—to assume or presuppose or simply assert—that there must have been a First Thing, an Unmoved Mover, a God.

But then, of course, we have to ask the question: where did God come from? Now notice, *we have no choice but to ask this question.* And why is that? Well, it's because we cannot imagine—we really cannot have the idea of—something that exists that wasn't caused by something else. Indeed, the claim that God exists—that there was an Unmoved Mover—is itself based precisely on the idea that everything that exists must have been caused to exist by something other than itself. The very idea of an Unmoved Mover presupposes the logic of cause and effect. But this means that it necessarily undermines itself.

Let's think this through. I know I'm beginning to repeat myself, which is going to happen sometimes, but I believe that's actually a good thing, and I'm hoping you'll agree that a little repetition can be extremely useful. So the claim that there was an Unmoved Mover assumes the idea of a causal chain wherein everything that exists must have been caused by something other than itself, something that preceded it in time. That's why people talk about an Unmoved Mover. The Unmoved Mover theory presupposes that the world is a world of cause and effect where nothing—absolutely nothing—arises simply and purely out of thin air. That's what the world is: a chain of cause and effect. But something had to get the chain going. Something had to, so to speak, knock down the first domino. And that's why you need the idea of Unmoved Mover. To start the chain in motion. So anyone who makes any claim about an Unmoved Mover is making a claim that is defended by, is internal to, the cause-and-effect manner of thinking that virtually all human beings share—except very small children and maybe some insane people.

But this same manner of thinking—the idea that everything that exists must be caused by something other than itself—makes it impossible for us to have the idea of an Unmoved Mover. For if there's an Unmoved Mover, then the Unmoved Mover exists; and if it exists, then, according to the logic of cause and effect, something must have caused it to exist; hence, it cannot have been unmoved at all. Something other than itself—something previous to itself—moved it. And of course, that other thing, the thing that moved the so-called Unmoved Mover, itself existed; as such, *it* must have been caused or moved by something previous to itself, and so on ad infinitum.

We're back to that ad infinitum stuff. The problem with ad infinitum—again—is that the logic of cause and effect requires that there was a beginning, a start. Something must have caused everything else. Something must have come first. Ad infinitum suggests that there was no beginning, hence—well—no cause. But if there was no cause, no beginning, how did things get moving in the first place? If you keep moving back and back and back, you still have to ask yourself—according to the logic of cause and effect—where it all began, what caused all of it to happen. We have to believe that something started it all. So the logic of cause and effect absolutely requires an Unmoved Mover. We can't do without it. But as we've just seen, the logic of cause and effect also absolutely rules out an Unmoved Mover—since if the Unmoved Mover existed, then something must have caused it to exist.

We're stuck.

Well then—you'll ask—how about faith? Given what I've just said, the logic of cause and effect rules out an Unmoved Mover. But without the Unmoved Mover, it's impossible to explain how the world could exist. So let's just forget about the logic of cause and effect and posit the existence of—have faith in—an Unmoved Mover. What's wrong with that?

We can begin to answer this question by acknowledging what's perhaps obvious, namely, that the faith thing is a really important part of religion. Indeed, it's probably the most important part of all. In a sense, faith is what religion is all about—though that's not quite as obvious as you might think.[3]

A particularly influential and admirably frank example of the faith idea is to be found, I'd say, in the version of Christianity that was proposed by St. Paul. Paul was actually an extremely interesting thinker, and I'm going to say a little more about him later on, in chapter 7. At this point, however, I'm still in the process of laying out the general problem—the problem with God—in its broad outlines. And so for now, all you need to know, or remember, is that the letters of St. Paul are almost certainly the oldest documents of the Christian bible, and this makes them awfully important. Indeed, in the early years of Christianity they played a central role in debates—sometimes angry, heated, even violent debates—about the real meaning of Christianity. And one could say without too much exaggeration that the Pauline version is the version that pretty much won out in the end. It became, so to speak, the official version.

Now St. Paul's view, grotesquely oversimplified, is that Christianity is fundamentally about faith—faith in God and in Jesus. This means that it's not fundamentally about obeying the law—for example, the law that God gave to Moses in the Ten Commandments. That's what some people thought way back then, but not Paul. Nor is it fundamentally about acquiring some deep, perhaps mystical knowledge of God's will. Again, that was a pretty popular view in the old days. But it wasn't Paul's. No, real Christianity, for Paul, is a matter neither of obedience nor of knowledge nor of insight nor of intuition but of pure, blind, irrational faith. And in fact, the more difficult it is to have faith in, say, Jesus—the more outlandish or ridiculous the thing is we're supposed to believe in—the better. The great English philosopher and statesman Francis Bacon, writing about sixteen hundred years after Paul, put the point nicely: "the more discordant, therefore, and incredible, the divine mystery is, the more honour is shown to God in believing it, and the nobler is the victory of faith."[4] It's pretty easy to believe, say, that the sun will rise tomorrow in the east. Anyone can believe that. It's easy to believe that a punch in the nose will cause pain. No problem there. Those kinds of beliefs don't take any effort; they involve no great existential commitment. But to believe really and truly in, say, miracles—things that seem utterly and entirely impossible, like turning water into wine or rising from the dead—that takes real faith. That takes, as we say, a leap of faith. A big leap. And according to St. Paul and Francis Bacon, that's what God really wants.

There are, however, problems with the idea of having faith in the existence of an Unmoved Mover. Remember, to begin with, that the entire idea of an Unmoved Mover is driven by the logic of cause and effect. The idea of "moving" just is the idea of causing. And so, to believe in an Unmoved Mover is to believe that the world is a matter of cause and effect—in which case, the Unmoved Mover, as something that exists, must itself have been caused by something other than itself, in which case it's not unmoved at all. In other words, it's hard to believe in an Unmoved Mover without believing in the universality of cause and effect, which, in turn, rules out the idea of an Unmoved Mover.

But why couldn't we say something like the following? Everything that exists must have been caused by something other than itself, *except* the Unmoved Mover. Let's call this the Exception Theory. That's what faith is all about: the Exception Theory. According to the Exception Theory, we're all governed by the logic of cause and effect, but we must nonetheless posit—have faith in, an irrational belief in—an exception. The exception is the Unmoved Mover. The Really, Really First Thing. God. Shall we call this the exception that proves the rule? Well, not exactly. Rather, it's the exception that argues against rules. The rules say that everything is a matter of cause and effect. So faith trumps, so to speak, the rules.

Of course, the logic of cause and effect makes it really hard to believe in an Unmoved Mover. But from the perspective of faith, that's exactly what you want. Because—remember—the harder it is to believe, the deeper the faith, and the deeper the faith, the better.

At least that's the Pauline view, and I would suggest, again, that Paul has put his finger on a lot of what the religious experience is all about.

The trouble with all this, I think, is pretty simple. I just don't know what it is that I'm supposed to have faith in. There's no concept of the thing in which I'm supposed to believe. And if I don't and can't have a concept of the thing in which I'm supposed to believe, then I simply can't believe in it. There's no "it" to believe in. Literally nothing. I can't believe in something unless I have an idea or image of what it is I'm suppose to believe in. And as I've said, there is no idea of an Unmoved Mover. There's no idea of something that absolutely must exist and, at the same time, absolutely cannot exist. That's a thought that I cannot have. So this means that it's something in which I cannot have faith. It's not really something at all. It's nothing. There is no there there.[5]

But wait a minute. Isn't it obvious that I *do* in fact have an idea or concept of an Unmoved Mover? Haven't I already said what it is? The Unmoved Mover is simply that which causes everything else but is itself uncaused. Why isn't that an idea? Maybe a difficult idea, maybe a silly idea, maybe the idea of miracle. But an idea, no?

In actual fact, no.

2

WHAT IN GOD'S NAME AM I DOING?

Before I try to explain why—before, that is, I attempt to prove to you that there is not and can never be a concept of an Unmoved Mover, hence of God—let me take a small step backward and say a few things about just what it is that I'm doing here. What am I up to? What's my plan? What's this little book really all about?

And the first thing I want to say is that I'm not doing theology. I'm not a theologian, and I don't pretend to be. You are not reading a theological treatise.

Now what do I mean by that? Well, basically I mean that, perhaps despite appearances, I'm not interested in formulating deep and subtle proofs of the existence or non-existence of God. In fact, I'm not even interested in formulating superficial and crude proofs of the existence or non-existence of God. That—the deep and subtle stuff, of course—is what theologians do, but it's not what I'm doing. Theologians spend a lot of time trying to demonstrate beyond any doubt—or, on occasion, to disprove beyond any doubt—the existence of God. Not me. That's not what I'm up to.

I should say, by the way, that I've actually read a fair amount of theology in my time. Wonderful stuff—often very difficult, very challenging. But the simple fact is that I'm not enough of an expert to offer my own theology. Indeed, I don't have one. I am, with respect to all of these questions, a layman; the book you are reading is nothing other than an attempt by one lay person to share his thoughts with other lay persons. And what this means, among other things, is that I cannot prove either the existence or nonexistence of God. Indeed, I really have no interest in trying to do so. That's not my project—for reasons that will become obvious to you, if they haven't already.

And when I say I'm not a theologian, I also mean that I won't be attempting to comment on or interpret any particular religious doctrine, not even St. Paul's. A lot of theologians do that as well. They try to explain what others have said about God; even more, they try to explain holy writings themselves. But that's not what I'm doing. I don't know what the Christian bible "really" means, any more than I know what, say, the Hebrew bible or the Koran or the Upanishads mean. Frankly, I don't have the brains or the background to figure any of that out. And believe me, I'm certainly not going to belittle people who spend their time doing it. Theological literature is often profound and massively intelligent, well worth studying. Some of the people who've done it—Thomas Aquinas, for example—are among the smartest people who've ever lived. And that sure isn't me. No false modesty here. Just the plain truth.

I'm also not purporting to say how things in the world actually are. Now this is important. I am not attempting to describe reality. Let me be even more specific: I'm not attempting to provide an account of the true, honest-to-goodness, underlying structure of the universe. I'm not doing what used to be called "metaphysics."[1] To be absolutely blunt, I don't claim to know the truth—at least no more than anyone else.

So what *am* I trying to do? Well, let's start with this: I'm trying to decide how it's possible for ordinary people—people like you and me, non-experts—to think about things in such a way that makes sense to us. Given some basic facts about how our minds seem to operate, what should we think if our thoughts are to be at least roughly coherent? How can we make sure that our thoughts and beliefs are, shall we say, not too crazy?

Actually, that's not quite it either. Or at least, that's not enough, not nearly. It doesn't really begin to describe what I'm up to. So let me tell a story that might help.

The other day, a friend said to me: "I think the Mariners will win the pennant this year." We had just watched a Mariners game—that's the Seattle Mariners, a major league baseball team—and they were awesome. My friend is a big Mariners fan, he's desperate for the Mariners to be successful, and we had just seen the team play a beautiful game. So he said what he said: "I think the Mariners will win the pennant." The problem is, I know quite well that my friend doesn't really believe what he just said. Not deep down. He doesn't believe it for a second. He said he thinks the Mariners will win the pennant—he actually had that thought and he expressed that thought in words—but in another sense he doesn't really think that at all. He has, let's say, two thoughts. One is the thought that he expressed out loud, the thought that the Mariners will win the pennant. But then there's the other thought, the thought he really believes. I know he believes the Mariners are actually terrible this year—which they are. They have absolutely no hitting and no bullpen, so it's bizarre to imagine them winning the pennant. My friend understands, deep down, that they have no chance. That's not the thought that he expressed at the moment when he said what he said, but if you asked me what he *really* thinks, that's the one I'd pick. That's his real belief, despite what he said.

There's often a big difference between the thoughts we sometimes express and the thoughts we really believe. The thoughts we really believe are the thoughts we would express if we—dare I say—thought about it a bit. Sometimes our mouths move faster than our brains; and sometimes certain parts of our brains move faster than other parts; and so what we say, or even what we consciously think, is often different from what we really think, from what we're really committed to, deep down.

What I'm trying to do in this book is figure out what we really think—whether or not we always say it or whether or not we're always conscious of it. And by "we," I mean you and me. Ordinary people. Or at least most ordinary people—pretty much everyone except very small children and maybe some insane people. I'm trying to explain what we should be saying if our words are to be consistent with our underlying beliefs. If we thought a bit more about our own real views, if we were careful to make sure that our conscious beliefs and the things we say were faithful to our innermost convictions and commitments, then what would we consciously think and what would we say? That's what I'm trying to discover.

In certain circles this is sometimes called philosophy.

Now that might seem scary. Or nerdy, or creepy, or irrelevant, or otherwise off-putting. But it's really none of those things. Because philosophy—at least the kind of philosophy I try to do—is, in a sense, pretty simple stuff. Philosophy, I'm going to say, is nothing other than the effort to uncover and bring to light our own ordinary, underlying beliefs so that what we actually say, and what we consciously think, is consistent with what we really think, deep down. And if that's what philosophy is, then yes indeed, I'm doing some philosophy here. But there's certainly nothing weird, remarkable, or out of the ordinary about it. Because the simple fact is that everyone's a philosopher. I mean that literally. Pretty much everyone. And I'm not trying to make some cutesy or sappy or New Agey point here. I'm being quite serious. Everyone does philosophy, fairly serious philosophy, pretty much on a regular basis. Including you.

To see why this might be the case—to see how you yourself are almost certainly a regular practitioner of philosophy, whether you're aware of it or not—let's think about, say, a talk radio show where people call in. And let's stick with the sports motif. Let's think about a sports radio talk show. Many years ago when I was driving a taxicab in New York City until two or three in the morning, sports talk radio kept me sane. Maybe.[2] Since then, I've always had—so to speak—a hate-love-hate relationship with talk radio. Hate-love-hate. That means hate wins two to one, but it's not all hate.

In any case, let's say the topic for today's show is: should Barry Bonds get into the Baseball Hall of Fame? Now even if you're not a sports fan at all—and provided you haven't been living in Antarctica for a good part of the last decade—you'll know that Barry Bonds, formerly an outfielder for the Pittsburgh Pirates and San Francisco Giants whose on-field exploits over a period of about twenty years were simply incredible, has been widely accused of cheating. Specifically, he's been accused of using steroids to improve his performance. None of those accusations has been proved, and no authoritative agency has officially determined—yet—that Bonds used performance-enhancing drugs.[3] Perhaps most importantly, Major League Baseball, the official governing body of the sport, has not formally declared that he broke the rules. But there is, let's face it, plenty of circumstantial evidence, so a lot of people believe that he did break the rules.

Now let's suppose those people are right. Let's suppose—just suppose—that Bonds did break the rules, and that he's been found guilty. So here we are, listening to sports talk radio, and people are calling in from everywhere and they're disagreeing. Ralph, for example, calls in from Bensonhurst and he's pretty steamed: it'd be a travesty, a real travesty, if Bonds, that bum, ever gets into the Hall of Fame. But Alice, who lives in Walla Walla, strongly disagrees: Barry's record is fantastic, amazing, incredible, so he should definitely be a Hall of Famer.

From the perspective of baseball, by the way, this is actually fairly important stuff. After all, 99.9 percent (or so) of major league players never get into the Hall. And that's 99.9 percent of *major league* players. If you count *all* baseball players—guys[4] who played in high school and in the Babe Ruth league and in your town's adult recreational league and so on—the number's more like 99.9999 percent. So getting into the Hall is pretty special. It's a big deal.

Notice, however, that when people like Ralph and Alice call in to talk about Barry Bonds, or about anything else, they're never just disagreeing. They're never simply taking different sides. They're doing something more. They're giving *reasons*. Indeed, that's what talk radio is all about. That's what makes it go. That's why we listen. Reasons. And what kind of reasons? Well, let's think about it. Ralph, let's assume, believes Barry shouldn't be in the Hall of Fame because, says Ralph, the Hall of Fame "is supposed to be the place that represents baseball at its best, in all respects." The Hall is a celebration of all the wonderful things about the game, and that includes not just playing well but also playing according to the rules, fair and square, honestly and with good sportsmanship. That's what it means to be a Hall of Famer. Alice, on the other hand, thinks Ralph is just wrong. The Hall of Fame, says Alice, "is supposed to be where you recognize the best players." Emphasize *players*. Period. Not citizens, not goody-two-shoes, not nice guys—just guys who could really play. Bonds may not have been Mr. Clean but he was an absolutely incredible player. So, says Alice, it's a no-brainer, nothing could be plainer, he should be a Hall of Famer.

But exactly what kinds of reasons are these? What kinds of reasons do people like Ralph and Alice offer? Well, look closely at what each of them in our hypothetical example has said. In each case they've told us what the Hall of Fame "is supposed to be." And when they say that, they're telling us what they think the Hall of Fame—and a Hall of Famer—really is, deep down. They're providing (partial) definitions of a thing, the thing we call the Hall of Fame. Of course, we have the Hall of Fame itself, the physical place in Cooperstown with its buildings and exhibits and all. But we also have an idea—a concept—of what it is, a concept of its essence, a concept of what makes the Hall of Fame the Hall of Fame. That's what Ralph and Alice are trying to get at.

There's more, however. Because both of them, Ralph and Alice, also assume this is a concept that, deep down, we share—all of us, at any rate, who think about and know about and care about the Hall of Fame. That, too, is implicit in the phrase "supposed to be." When someone says the Hall of Fame is "supposed to be" this, that, or the other thing, "supposed to be" means not only that's what it is. It also means that when you think about it, when you hear the arguments, you'll realize that that's what you, like the rest of us, really understood all along. You just weren't fully aware of it.

And that, I want to suggest, is pretty much what philosophy is all about. No more, no less. It is the attempt to unearth and bring to light what we already really know, you and I—to discover our own beliefs, deep down, about what some particular thing is, beliefs that we're not always consciously aware of but that are ours nonetheless.

But exactly how do people like Ralph and Alice—and you and I—make their arguments? How do they proceed? What kind of evidence do we use? Now that, of course, is a complicated question, but a lot of the time we use examples. So Ralph might say, "Look, as most of us already know, Pete Rose, a great player, is not in the Hall of Fame, and that's because he broke the rules—he gambled on baseball, a big no-no—so if we keep him out, we should keep Bonds out too." To which Alice might reply, "That's absurd, because, as most of us already know, Gaylord Perry, another great player, also broke the rules—he freely admits he threw spitballs when he pitched, another big no-no—but since he's in the Hall of Fame and nobody wants to kick him out, why not Bonds?" In each such case, the examples are designed to remind us of things we already know but may have forgotten or ignored, thereby forcing us to see the deeper implications—the underlying logic—of our shared knowledge. And so the argument goes, all night long, example after example, caller after caller—while some poor cabbie, a latter-day version of the old me, is maneuvering his hack around and through the streets of Gotham with the radio on, trying to stay sane.

Everyone, each of us, makes these kinds of arguments all the time: your doctor and your auto mechanic, your tax advisor and your butcher, your op-ed columnist and the person who does your nails. Every one of us is a philosopher. Now we might not all be equally good philosophers. After all, when it comes to philosophy, most of us are not professionals. Which means most of us don't do philosophy as systematically or with the same rigor as someone who's been trained in philosophy and who does it for a living. Philosophy is one of those things—like being a doctor or an auto mechanic or a manicurist—that can be learned, and that can be done well or badly. Of course, presumably philosophy is something that I myself have learned to do. I do it for a living, and so presumably I do it reasonably well. That's, in part, why I've written this book—not because I'm an expert on God and religion, which I'm not, but because I've been taught to think philosophically. But always remember, bad philosophy is still philosophy.

So you, readers, are philosophers all. And by the way, if you don't like my sports example, that's not a problem. Instead of Hall of Famer, just substitute, say, Oscar-winning movie. Or presidential timber. Or ideal spouse. Or perfect apple pie. In all such cases, we can, if the occasion arises, dig down, way down, and try to discover our own shared beliefs about what the thing in question really is, beliefs to which we are deeply committed even if we're often not fully aware of them. Of course, the list of particular things we might think about in this way is virtually infinite: movies, presidents, spouses, apple pie, the Hall of Fame, and pretty much everything else. But surely the list also includes God. Deep down, what do we *really* think when we talk about—when we say we believe in or don't believe in or don't yet have evidence about—the existence of God?

Philosophy it is, then. That's what I'm doing, and I'm not doing it alone. I'm doing it with you. We're in this together—comrades in the pursuit of philosophical wisdom.

But now for another disclaimer: in this book, I am not—repeat *not*—claiming to be saying anything startlingly new, not in philosophy or in anything else. This is extremely important. If I'm doing philosophy—and I think I am—I am nonetheless and most emphatically not pretending to be making an original contribution to the philosophical literature.

Now I have to say that, in actual fact, I'm really not certain if I'm making an original contribution or not. I'm pretty darn sure I'm not, though I suppose it's possible. But it also doesn't matter. Because making an original contribution—a brand new, previously unknown philosophical argument—is just not what I'm after. I have no such ambitions and certainly no such pretensions.

This is actually a bit complicated. It's complicated, in part, by the simple fact that in thinking about God and other, similar things, there's rarely if ever anything new under the sun. At least not completely new. Most of the ideas we come up with have been thought of before, by someone and in some form. And what this means is that claims to being truly original are really pretty hard to justify. That's not a problem for me—thank God—because I'm making no such claims and have no interest in doing so. That's just not what this book is about. But of course, the whole situation is made even more complicated by the fact that my goal, as I've said, is to uncover and reconstruct thoughts that all or most of us already have, deep down, even if we're not aware of them. I'm trying to make explicit—to make clear, obvious, and evident—things that we, you and I, already know implicitly but that we, you and I, don't generally think about, don't often talk about, and aren't particularly conscious of. But notice. If we all already know this stuff, even only subconsciously, then I'm really not saying anything new at all; and even more, if we already know this stuff, even only subconsciously, then it's also highly likely that someone else, somewhere along the line, has already found out about it and has written it up.[5] Indeed, it would be a bit odd if that weren't the case. So the bottom line: I would never say with a straight face that the arguments I'm presenting here are brand new. I would never claim to be breaking completely new ground—philosophical or otherwise. That's not what I'm trying to do.

You might be interested to know, by the way, that I actually have tried to break new ground—new philosophical ground—elsewhere, in other books I've written, books that deal with subjects, especially political subjects, very different from this one. I have, in other words, tried to make genuinely original arguments—to make arguments that are both true and that have not been made before. But not here. That's not what this book is about.

So then—you'll ask—why in God's name did I write this book in the first place? If I'm not saying anything original, why am I saying anything at all? What am I really up to?

And the answer is that even if most or all of my arguments have already been made before, I'm also *not* convinced that they've always been well stated. Indeed, it's possible they've never been well stated. But the more important point for us: they certainly have been well stated recently.

In the past few years, a number of books have been written about God, both for and against. Some of these books have been best sellers. But none of them has made the arguments I'm making here; or if they've made those arguments, they haven't made them with a whole lot of clarity. And that's a real problem. Because the authors of these books keep making mistakes—the same mistakes, over and over again. And I really am talking about all sides of the debate—the pro-God side, the anti-God side, and the fence-sitting side. They all keep saying things—often the same things, despite their disagreements—that they just shouldn't be saying. And they wouldn't be saying those things if they took the kinds of arguments I'm making more seriously, at least to the point of making sure those arguments are well stated. Because if they did that, they'd see that some of the things they're saying are actually out of whack with what they, and the rest of us, really think, deep down.

And when I say "well stated," what do I mean? Well, basically I mean stated in a way that's useful for readers who don't have PhDs in philosophy or religion—which is to say readers who have chosen not to spend years and years mastering the arcane, technical, esoteric language of academic philosophy or scholastic theology. I'm talking about making very important and sometimes complicated problems intelligible to literate nonspecialists. And I'm also talking about not making complicated problems even more complicated than they already are. Because in the end, the ideas I'm presenting—ideas that in some sense most of us already share, even if we're not always aware of it—just aren't all that peculiar.

So here, in somewhat different words, is what I'm trying to do in a nutshell: I'm trying to present what may well be old arguments in a form that's direct, straightforward, jargon-free, and persuasive—arguments that most of us already know, at least deep down, but that we rarely, if ever, say out loud, even to ourselves.

And why am I doing this? Basically, I'm doing it because I think it's good to know what we really think. I'm doing it because too many people too often forget about—they fail to think about—their own beliefs. I'm doing it because most of the other recent books on God haven't done it—and the fact that they haven't done it has actually made matters a little bit worse. So I'm trying to get us back in touch with ourselves, with our own innermost convictions. Call it a kind of consciousness-raising. If you think something—if you really, really believe something deep down and are committed to it so that it informs what you do and how you live—it's probably a good idea to know what it is.

It's an especially good idea to know what it is when sometimes—or often—you say things and think things and act on the basis of things that are contrary to what you really believe.

From what I said a moment ago, by the way, you shouldn't conclude that I'm totally against arcane, technical, esoteric language. I'm not. In fact, I've sometimes used such language myself, and, like it or not, it's often necessary. In the same way that many important, complex arguments in, say, physics or math can't be stated with real accuracy and depth without relying on highly abstruse modes of expression, so too in philosophy. But happily, my goal here doesn't require this at all. It doesn't require technical language. In fact, it requires exactly the opposite. Rather than present some new great discovery in philosophy—rather than pursue the problem of God in a way that explores all the subtle nuances and connections, all the contexts and minute implications—my purpose, rather, is to help us put our own ordinary thoughts in order, to help us understand our own intuitions, yours and mine, to help us distinguish the things that we sometimes say and sometimes appear to believe from the things that we really believe, deep down. And doing this requires plain, ordinary language. The goal is not originality. The goal is clarity.[6]

That's my game. Clarity. Figuring out clearly what we—you and I—really think, even if, or especially if, we're not fully aware of what we really think. So that we can be in touch with our innermost convictions. And so that we can make sense.

But before moving on, I'm afraid I do need to say just one more thing about what I'm doing here. Can't be avoided.

As I've just indicated, sometimes there's a big difference between the thoughts we express or consciously think and the thoughts we really believe in, deep down. But sometimes—occasionally—the thoughts that we express or consciously think aren't simply out of whack with our true thoughts. Sometimes the thoughts we express or consciously think are, in fact, not really thoughts at all. Sometimes our words—the things we say—express not thoughts but gobbledygook. Nonsense. Incoherence. Gibberish. Noise. I'm not even sure what to call them. But whatever they are, they're out of whack with our real thoughts not just because they're different from our real thoughts but because they're just not thoughts at all.

Now my friend's thought—his fleeting thought—that the Mariners will win the pennant, that's a real thought, an honest-to-goodness thought. It's not something he believes deep down, because he really knows that it won't happen. But it is, despite this, a thought—a terrible thought, a thought that's wrong, a thought that's inconsistent with his own way of thinking, with what he really believes, but a thought nonetheless. If he were truly to believe in that thought, I'd know exactly what he was believing in. I could identify clearly just what the thought is. It's the thought that the Mariners will win the pennant, meaning simply that at the end of the season they will have won more games than any other team in the American League.[7] Won't happen. But I know what it is that won't happen. The concept makes perfect sense. And so when I say my friend doesn't really believe this, I know what the "this" is that he doesn't believe.

But there are other things that appear to be thoughts—things that we say and seem to think—that aren't really thoughts at all. I want to say that God is one of those. I want to say that there is no thought there. And therefore, there's nothing there to believe in. There is no concept.

This is pretty important, so let me say it in another way. If my friend thinks about things, he'll realize that the thought that the Mariners will win the pennant is in fact something he doesn't believe. With respect to the Mariners winning the pennant, he's a non-believer. He expresses an honest-to-goodness thought—that the Mariners will win the pennant—but he rejects that thought as something that he doesn't really think. I want to say that God is not like this at all. I want to say that there is, in fact, no concept of God—no idea or no thought of God. And from this I want to say not only is it impossible to believe in God but also impossible to disbelieve in God. Just as there's nothing to affirm, so is there nothing to deny. The question of the existence of God is a non-question. It's a question that's impossible to answer because impossible to ask.

Now before we finally get on with things—which we will, I promise, very soon—you might want to know a bit more about me, about who I am. You might be curious. That would be only natural, I suppose. But the simple fact is that it really doesn't matter. Let me repeat that: it doesn't matter *who* I am. I'm talking about me. Your author. The first-person narrator. Doesn't matter. I hope I'm not disappointing you, but you really don't need to know anything about me. The only thing that matters here is what I'm saying. What matters is my argument—which I think is right, and which I think you should think is right.

So it doesn't matter that I was raised in a family that was utterly and avowedly secular and that, at the same time, made no bones about the fact that we were Jews, through and through. It doesn't matter that one day my father, when he was a fourteen-year-old boy living in Szombathely—a provincial capital about midway between Vienna and Budapest on the Hungarian side of the border—decided he wasn't going to synagogue ever again and so, defying *his* father, skipped services and spent the afternoon at a (very public) downtown *conditorei* where he gorged himself on *dobos torta* or *turos retes* or some other decadent pastry. It doesn't matter that my brother was bar mitzvahed, but that I, eight years later, was given a choice and gracefully declined—to the great relief of everyone. It doesn't matter that I went to a Catholic college, the only Jew, I believe, in an undergraduate student body of eight or nine thousand—an avatar of multiculturalism before its time! It doesn't matter that my wife, as a fifteen-year-old girl in Quebec, did something quite similar to what my father had done thirty years earlier in Hungary—except that she skipped not synagogue but Mass.

It doesn't matter that I'm a philosopher—a teacher/scholar—who is interested, above all, in trying to be consistent and coherent. It doesn't matter that I'm one of those geeks whose professional life is devoted to the attempt, against all the odds, to make arguments that are airtight—which isn't easy, believe me. It doesn't matter that I am, for better or worse, committed to persuading others not through the beauty of words or the glitter of images but through the strength of reason and the cogency of evidence.

It really doesn't matter.

And it probably doesn't even matter that I cannot abide—I hate—mumbo-jumbo.

Now I should say that I use that term advisedly, and not without a certain affection. *Mumbo-jumbo*. A wonderful term, really. It's true that other terms suggest themselves. *Baloney* might be one. *BS* might be another (and note that for every bull there's a horse). Also *hogwash* (and its peculiar variant, *eyewash*), *nonsense*, *garbage*, a *crock* (of this, that or the other thing), *bilge* (especially if you have a maritime background), and *twaddle*. I've already mentioned *gibberish* and *gobbledygook*. But let's not forget *poppycock* and *tommyrot*. And oh yes, *balderdash*. What a terrific word, balderdash.

Now mumbo-jumbo certainly is balderdash. But the great thing about mumbo-jumbo is that it's a particular kind of balderdash.

Mumbo-jumbo is balderdash all dressed up in exotic clothes, in elaborate, mystical garb, as though there were, underneath the layers and layers of silk and satin and sequined taffeta, some kind of deep, arcane, hidden but very profound truth—a glorious secret—when, in fact, there's nothing there at all. Mumbo-jumbo describes a certain way of being wrong and, more particularly, a certain kind of gibberish. It's not a matter of just being wrong. It's a matter of being pretentiously wrong. And it's not a matter of simple gibberish. It's gibberish with attitude.

I'm not a big fan of mumbo-jumbo. I get really frustrated when people make decisions based on mumbo-jumbo. Seems bizarre to me. But I get even more frustrated when people make important decisions that affect *other* people (especially me!) based on mumbo-jumbo—decisions about the law, about right and wrong, about war and peace. I'm not crazy, for example, about living in a world where it's impossible, simply and completely impossible, to become President of the United States unless you believe in—or at least can plausibly claim to believe in—the mumbo-jumbo that we call God. And I get equally—yes, equally—frustrated when I realize that the ritualistic mumbo-jumbo of God seems to be counterbalanced only by the equally ritualistic mumbo-jumbo of atheism and the seemingly more benign but, in a strange way, even more insidious and corrupting mumbo-jumbo of agnosticism. It is, I have to say, a mumbo-jumbo world out there.

I get frustrated by the fact that what we all know deep down is something that we rarely, if ever, say. We know what's going on. We just don't permit ourselves to acknowledge it. And so we embrace mumbo-jumbo. We let our lives—and the lives of others—be driven by the mumbo and the jumbo of it all.

It probably doesn't matter that, for whatever it's worth, this little book is borne of deep, abiding, gnawing, gut-wrenching, hold-it-inside-but-wanna-scream-out-loud frustration—frustration with a world that really ought to, and deep down does, know better.

It's impossible—as I say—to believe in God, and it's also impossible to disbelieve in God. Just as there's nothing to affirm, so is there nothing to deny. The question of the existence of God is a non-question. It's a question that's impossible to answer because impossible to ask.

To show why, I need to do several things. First, I need to explain what I mean by "impossible." What's the nature of the impossibility that I'm describing? Second, I need to say a lot more about atheism and agnosticism. Given what I've said so far, shouldn't I be an atheist? After that, I need to talk some more about faith. Why isn't faith a simple solution to all our problems? In addition, I need to look more closely at the logic of cause and effect. Are we all really and necessarily committed to thinking about the world in that way? I also have to address the idea of mystery. Can't we just accept the idea that God's a mystery, but a mystery that exists nonetheless? Finally, I need to say something about hope, since the account I'm proposing is, believe it or not, the most hopeful and cheery account that anyone could imagine—way more hopeful and way more cheery than anything religion has to offer. Indeed, stay tuned. I think I've got good news for you.

3

THE IMPOSSIBLE DREAM

It's impossible to believe in God and also impossible to disbelieve in God, because the question of God is impossible to ask.

So what do I mean by "impossible"?

Now different things can be impossible in different ways. Or rather: there are different kinds of impossibility. Let's start with a very simple example. It's impossible—just impossible—for me to dunk a basketball. And there's nothing, absolutely nothing, I can do about it. This, by the way, is another one of the things that's enormously frustrating for me. I'd like nothing better than to be able to dunk. But I'm sixty-three years old, just under six feet tall, the basket is ten feet high, and I just can't get up there. Worse, I never could. I used to be fully six feet tall—I've lost a good inch over time, my disks not being as juicy as they once were—but even at my physical best, when I was nineteen or twenty, I just couldn't jump that high. I could grab the rim with my hand—not too bad, but not good enough.

You might say I was too short. But height wasn't the only problem. I played schoolyard basketball a few times with a fellow from the next town over. His name was Calvin Murphy. Calvin was actually an inch or so shorter than me, but he could dunk. In fact, he could dunk with ease. No problem at all. He was shorter than me, but he had some kind of physical ability—a God-given talent!—that I didn't have. So height wasn't the whole story.

I should say, as an aside, that Calvin Murphy's physical superiority to me wasn't just a matter of jumping ability. It was pretty much everything. A high school All-American basketball player, he went on to Niagara University where he led the nation in scoring. From there he went to the Houston Rockets of the NBA and, despite being so short, became an All-Star and, eventually, a member of the Basketball Hall of Fame—indeed, arguably one of the greatest players inch-for-inch in the history of the game.

In any case, what was possible, indeed easy, for Calvin was—and certainly still is—simply impossible for me.

Let's call this Physical Impossibility.

Suppose I have a string and I want to tie it from one end of my room to the other. The string is ten feet long. The room is, from end to end, eleven feet. Try as I might, there's no way I can tie the string from one end of my room to the other. It won't reach. It's Physically Impossible.

It's Physically Impossible for things (on earth) to fall upward; gravity won't allow it. It's Physically Impossible for an ant to defeat an elephant in a fair fight; the elephant's too big. It's Physically Impossible to make beef stew out of sand and nothing else; no beef, no goulash.

But now consider a slightly different kind of case. Santa Claus, I want to suggest, is impossible. At least, Santa Claus as he's always been described. I'm talking about the entire Santa thing: the beard and the belly, the sled and the deer, the elves and the North Pole, the whole shebang. Just flat-out impossible. To begin with, reindeer can't fly. Can't be done. Too heavy, no wings. Moreover, Santa can't fit down most chimneys—any more than I can dunk. He's too chubby. Or perhaps it's that chimneys are too thin. Either way, no dice. And of course, it's impossible that one jolly old man in a red suit could collect the wish lists of millions and millions of children, buy or make or otherwise acquire millions and millions of toys, pack all of those millions and millions of toys onto a single sled, and then fly around the world and distribute all those toys—via millions and millions of narrow chimneys—to all those children, making sure the right child always gets the right toy, all in a single evening while, in the process, eating millions and millions of cookies and drinking millions and millions of glasses of milk.

All of this is Physically Impossible, just like my dunking and just like my string. But there's a difference. The difference is that while I exist, and dunking exists, and the string exists, and my room exists, Santa doesn't exist. In his case, the Physical Impossibility is such that we don't believe in the existence of the thing itself. Except for little children, we are all to Santa as atheists are—or, rather, claim to be—to God. With respect to Santa, we're nonbelievers. We're not a-theists; we're a-Santa-ists. We don't believe in the existence of Santa, at least as usually depicted, because we don't believe that Santa is physically possible. Here, Physical Impossibility doesn't just rule out the possibility of something happening; it rules out the possibility of some entity actually existing.[1]

There are, to be sure, other reasons we don't believe in Santa. One good one is that we've never seen him. Of course, we've seen countless imitations—on the street corner, as part of the Thanksgiving Day Parade, in the movies, in the department store (perhaps not too far from the column of dominoes waiting to be knocked over)—but we've never seen the real one. The fact that we've never seen the real Santa, however, doesn't in itself mean Santa's impossible. We've never seen the Abominable Snowman or Bigfoot or the Loch Ness Monster, and I'm not certain those things are impossible. We generally don't believe in the existence of the Abominable Snowman or Bigfoot or Nessie, but that's because none of them has been seen. If they existed, they would probably have been observed from time to time. Every so often they'd pop up. Every so often we'd get real good footage of them—not a grainy, shadowy, homemade tape but some honest-to-goodness Hi-Def. Hasn't happened. So their complete and total absence (so far) from view inclines us to doubt that they're there. Nonetheless, I can imagine they *might* be there. Even though they're almost certainly not there, they could, possibly, be. But Santa isn't like the Abominable Snowman or Bigfoot or Nessie. He's not simply unseen. He's unseen because it's Physically Impossible for him—the Santa with the reindeer and the sled and the toys and the chimneys—to exist. So our non-belief in Santa is actually way stronger than our non-belief in the Abominable Snowman, Bigfoot, or Nessie. You can't believe in the existence of something if you know that it can't possibly exist. Not if you're sane. And an adult.

But there's still another, very different kind of impossibility, not at all like my dunking or Santa's existing. Consider this case. It is impossible—completely, entirely, eternally impossible—for there to be a triangle whose internal angles don't add up to 180 degrees. No such thing. (Now bear in mind, I'm operating here within Euclidean premises. More on this later—I promise.) Every triangle that has ever been or that ever could be has three internal angles that add up to no more and no less than 180 degrees. There are no exceptions and there can be no exceptions. Exceptions are impossible. If something exists whose internal angles add up to more or less than 180 degrees, then it's not a triangle. A triangle is a plane figure—a three-sided polygon (in flat, not curved, space; again, bear with me)—formed by connecting three points not in a straight line by straight-line segments. Every such figure has three and only three internal angles and those angles add up to exactly 180 degrees, no more, no less. Anything—for example, any plane figure—that does not have three angles that add up to 180 degrees is not a triangle. It's impossible for any such figure to be a triangle.

This doesn't seem to be a matter of Physical Impossibility, like my dunking or even like Santa. It's not a matter of strength or leaping ability or distance or the presence or absence of wings on certain kinds of animals or the ability of one man to make millions and millions of deliveries in a single night. It's something different. Let's call it Conceptual Impossibility.

A triangle is really a concept, an idea. We can create physical approximations of that concept. We can draw triangles with pencil and paper. It's true that, at least as things currently stand, we can probably never draw an absolutely, microscopically perfect triangle. The very finest and most accurate drawing tools will almost certainly have some infinitesimal degree of inaccuracy; and so it's probably—arguably—Physically Impossible to draw an absolutely and completely perfect triangle. But we certainly can and do have the concept of a triangle. It's a simple concept that most of us are quite comfortable with. However, it is Conceptually

Impossible—not Physically Impossible, but Conceptually Impossible—for anyone at anytime and in any place to have the idea of a triangle whose internal angles add up to either more or less than 180 degrees. There is no such idea, no such concept.

God, I want to suggest, is Conceptually Impossible, roughly in the same way.

Before I say why, let me first provide yet a different kind of case that might turn out to be helpful—in part because the example of the triangle, though extremely useful in some respects, is, for reasons already hinted at, maybe not the best example.

Suppose I ask you the following question: how much does justice weigh in ounces and pounds or, if you'd rather, in grams and kilograms? Justice—understood as a moral quality, a characteristic of policies or actions or dispositions or arrangements that has something to do with fairness, evenhandedness, honesty, integrity, ethics. For example: today's tax system is (or isn't) an embodiment of justice. Or: Oliver Wendell Holmes had (or lacked) the virtue of justice. Or again: when the home team won the game, justice was (or wasn't) served.

So how much does justice weigh in ounces and pounds? If I asked you such a question, you'd think there was something wrong with me. Justice doesn't weigh anything in ounces and pounds. Now let me state that more clearly. I'm not saying that justice weighs zero. Justice does not weigh zero. The point is not that justice is weightless. It's not. An astronaut in space with zero gravity—now *that's* weightless. But not justice. Rather, justice is simply not the kind of thing you weigh. You can weigh an astronaut, even one that doesn't weigh anything. But the concept of weight—and I'm talking about physical weight, not metaphorical weight like the "weight" of the argument I'm making—such a concept simply doesn't apply to justice.

And what this means is that the concept of "justice weighing something in ounces and pounds" is a concept that we cannot have, a concept that does not and cannot exist. There is and can be no such concept. It's Conceptually Impossible.

Of course there are tons and tons (no pun intended) of other important things that are exactly like justice in this respect. I've already alluded to some of them in passing. In ounces and pounds, how much does ethics weigh? Or fairness or honesty or integrity? We can go on and on with such examples. And we certainly don't have to limit ourselves to weight. In feet and inches—or, if you'd rather, in meters and centimeters—exactly how long is love? Or beauty? Or courage? Three inches long? A foot? A mile? Ten thousand miles? A millimeter? What's longer in feet and inches: courage or the state of Oklahoma? The question makes no sense. And of course, our examples don't have to be limited to good things. What's the circumference in feet, or the volume in cubic centimeters, of evil or deceit or nastiness?

And again: let's not confuse physical weight with metaphorical weight. We might want to say that integrity is more "weighty" than courage, but when we say that, what we really mean is that the quality of integrity is, for some (presumably moral) reason, more important than the quality of being courageous. But that's just wordplay. Sometimes "weight" is used as a metaphor for "important." The weight that I've been talking about, on the other hand, is not a euphemism for important. I've been talking about real physical weight. Ounces, pounds, grams, kilos. If we ask how much an apple weighs or how much I weigh or how much an oxygen atom weighs or how much the earth weighs—and if we're talking about physical weight—these are intelligible questions. They are, in principle, answerable. If we want to know how much an apple weighs, we can put it on a scale. That's what we do in the supermarket every day. But if we want to know how much integrity weighs—in ounces and pounds—how would we answer that question? Exactly what would we put on the scale?

Now you might think: well Joe is a person of integrity, so let's put Joe on the scale. But of course, what you'd be doing there is weighing Joe's body—his physical body. You wouldn't be weighing his integrity.

We also don't have to limit ourselves to the kinds of moral or other personal qualities that I've mentioned so far. How large in ounces and pounds is pi? I mean the number pi. Notice that pi is, indeed, a number, and a fairly precise one at that. (Though that precision has its limits. Pi is, after all, an irrational number.) We know, for example, that pi is approximately twenty-two divided by seven, and we know exactly how much larger twenty-two divided by seven is than twenty-one divided by seven. It's one seventh larger, no more, no less. But to ask how much pi itself weighs in ounces and pounds is to ask something ridiculous. And it's equally ridiculous to ask the same question of even simpler things, say the number three. How much does three weigh? I don't mean three apples or three oxygen atoms. I'm talking about plain old three, all by itself. Again, we know that three is exactly one more than two and one less than four. But in terms of weight, this is usually not helpful. If we know exactly how much more three oxygen atoms weigh than two oxygen atoms, that's only because the weight of oxygen atoms is constant. But if we want to know how much more three apples weigh than two, we can't know until we weigh them, because individual apples have different weights. Indeed, it's easily possible for two apples to weigh more than three apples, depending on the apples. The fact of three—in and of itself—doesn't have weight.

Please keep in mind: it's not that three—or justice or love or pi—are very, very light. It's not that their weight is zero pounds and zero ounces. That's not what's going on here. Rather, it's that these things are the kinds of things for which the concept of weight simply doesn't apply at all. Please note, further, that these same things, to which weight (as well as physical height, width, length) doesn't apply, nonetheless play a hugely important role in our lives. Who could deny that three is an important part of what makes, say, the Three Little Pigs or the Three Blind Mice or the Three Musketeers what they are? Who could deny—rationally—that the area of a circle is pi times the squared radius? Who could deny that some people have courage and others don't, or that some outcomes are just and others aren't, or that there's a difference between love and lust, or that much hangs on the opposition between good and evil?

It's impossible that courage or love or fairness or pi or three could have physical weight. Impossible. This is not Physical Impossibility. It's not like the impossibility of me dunking a basketball. It's more like the impossibility of a triangle (in Euclidean space) whose internal angles add up to more or less than 180 degrees. It's a Conceptual Impossibility. It describes an idea that we simply cannot have. It is impossible to find—or even to look for—the physical weight of justice in ounces and pounds because it is impossible to have a concept of justice that has physical weight.

If you ask how much justice weighs in ounces and pounds, you're asking a question that's impossible to ask. Indeed, there is no question. It's not that the question is hard or even impossible to answer. It's that the question just doesn't make any sense at all. It really cannot be asked. What seems to be a question isn't really a question. And this is because there is no such idea as justice having weight. There is no concept there.

Of course, you can utter grammatically correct sentences that end in question marks and thus *seem* to be asking questions. That's easy. I can utter the following: "So how does pi—twenty-two divided by seven—taste? Is it sweet, salty, or sour?" (I'm talking about pi, not pie.) Or I can say: "Do the internal angles of love have more or less degrees than the internal angles of a triangle?" Or I can say: "What's more courageous, an oxygen atom or an apple?" (You can see from these examples, by the way, that I've only scratched the surface of Conceptual Impossibility.) The point, however, is simple: the fact that you've uttered some words that produce a grammatically correct sentence that ends in a question mark doesn't mean that you've asked a real question. By the same token, the fact that you've purported to use a concept doesn't mean you've really used one. The idea of pi having a flavor or of love having internal angles measurable in degrees or of an atom having courage—in each case there really is no such idea.

Another example: three—the number three itself—is not odorless. There are plenty of odorless things (odorless liquids for example). But three is not one of them. We can ask if water is odorless; we can ask if a hunk of Camembert cheese is odorless; we can ask if Raid is odorless. These questions make sense. But we can't ask this about three. And that's because three is not odorless. Of course, three is not only not odorless. It's also not odored. It is neither odored nor odorless. The concept of odor doesn't apply. You can try to smell water, just like you can try to smell a hunk of Camembert cheese. But try smelling three. I dare you. What would you do? Not only is there no such idea as three having or not having an odor. There can never, ever be such an idea. And so too with tasty or tasteless pi, or angled or angle-less love, or courageous or cowardly apples. There are no such ideas.

In this respect, Physical Impossibility is very different from Conceptual Impossibility—and that's crucial, because God is an example not of Physical but of Conceptual Impossibility.

I can imagine a world in which I would be able to dunk a basketball. I can have that idea. It wouldn't be the world I'm living in. The world would have to be different from the one I know. But I can imagine—I can have the idea of, I can dream up—such a world. Indeed, it actually wouldn't have to be that much different.

For example, I can imagine a world in which we had developed new training techniques—new ways to build muscles and tendons and ligaments—a world in which I would be able to take advantage of those techniques and, as a result, be able to dunk. It wouldn't be such a big change. At least not when I was nineteen or twenty. Remember, in those days I could grab the rim. Just a few more inches and—slam! That's all it would have taken. It's hardly fanciful to imagine new methods of training leading to somewhat better results.

Indeed, this kind of thing seems to happen all the time. It's almost certain that training techniques sometimes really do get better and that the performance of athletes sometimes improves accordingly. The fact that new records are constantly being broken in track-and-field might mean that people are getting bigger and stronger, but it probably also reflects better methods of preparation.

Or maybe I can have the idea of a world in which I could dunk not because of new training methods but because someone discovered a new way to jump—a new style of jumping. That may seem far-fetched, but in fact such things are hardly unheard of. A very famous and quite wonderful example occurred in high jumping itself—not jumping to dunk a basketball but the sport of jumping over a bar. In the early 1960s, a young man named Dick Fosbury, hanging around the track in Corvallis, Oregon, invented a whole new method of high jumping. Instead of scissoring his legs over the bar, or instead of rolling over the bar with his face and stomach facing the ground, he jumped over it with his back to the ground. They called it the Fosbury Flop. It was an inspirational discovery, a discovery of sheer genius. To the eye it seemed weird, bizarre, awkward. As he soared over the bar, Fosbury looked like an undulating snake floating in midair. But the technique worked. In fact, the results were astonishing. Without the Flop, Dick Fosbury was nothing special as a high jumper. Very ordinary. With the Flop, he won an Olympic gold medal. Within a very short time, every high jumper of any consequence switched over to the Fosbury Flop. It's now universal. You can simply jump higher that way.

There are many other examples. In basketball, someone at some point—the origins are highly disputed—invented the jump shot. Instead of shooting the ball while your feet are on the floor, you jump up in the air and then shoot the ball, which means you're shooting from a higher position than before and so it's harder for your opponent to block the shot. In the old days, no one took a jump shot. It didn't exist. Now, everyone does. It's a much better way to shoot. A new method led to vastly improved performance. In baseball, there are those who claim that the astonishing number of home runs hit by Mark McGuire, Sammy Sosa and, yes, our friend Barry Bonds in the late 1990s and early 2000s reflected not so much—or not exclusively—the effect of steroids or a lively ball but something called the rotational style of hitting, a new way to swing a bat that allegedly creates more power.

The point is that we can imagine other worlds in which what was Physically Impossible becomes very possible indeed. These are coherent, intelligible ideas. The world can change in a number of ways. And when it changes, it becomes—if only slightly—a different world. For one thing, we might simply discover something new about the world, something we didn't know before. Long ago, it seemed impossible to sail around the world, since the world was flat. Then we discovered it was round, and now we take worldwide cruises for granted (if we can afford them). For another, we might actually create something new in the world, and so what was in fact impossible now becomes entirely possible. Until very recently, humans couldn't create flying machines, though not for lack of effort. Now we can, and the world is a different place.[2] In the early 1800s, it would have been impossible—Physically Impossible—to get from the Atlantic coast to the Pacific coast in less than a month. Now—depending on weather and flight schedules—we can do it in four or five hours. (Of course, sometimes these changes aren't always for the best. We invented the nuclear bomb, and the world certainly is a different place because of it.)

Because we can imagine our world being different from what it is, we can also imagine fantastic, imaginary, strange and seemingly alien worlds that really don't seem possible at all. The history of the real world actually changing before our very eyes inspires us to imagine all kinds of other changes. Of course, that's what fantasy and science fiction are all about. We can imagine worlds run by sorcerers or magicians, or worlds in which people use "transporters" to move instantly from one place to a different and very distant place, or worlds populated by creatures from another planet whose powers far transcend our own.

We can conceive things that are, or appear to be, Physically Impossible. And in part, this is because the very idea of Physical Impossibility is, as we know from history, changeable.

I think we can even imagine a world in which Santa Claus exists—*the* Santa Claus, with the reindeer, the sleigh, and the millions and millions of toys. Of course, we already have the concept of Santa, by which I mean the Santa we all know and love—Physically

Impossible, at least for now, but conceptually unproblematic. But more, we already have at least a rough idea of how the world would have to change in order for Santa to exist, not simply conceptually but physically.

Now you'll think I've really gone off the deep end. Santa exist? Well, no. I'm not saying that's really possible. Not quite. But consider:

Suppose you're Aristotle. Suppose it's 343 BCE, and you're sitting around the Academy in Athens with your colleagues and students—maybe including Alexander soon-to-be-the Great (though this is actually highly unlikely, since young Alexander probably studied with Aristotle in Macedonia, not in Athens)—when someone shows up and claims there will come a day when folks will be able to sit right there in Athens, under the shadow of the Parthenon, not far from the Areopagus, hard by the Aegean, a stone's throw from the Piraeus, and in real time watch—live!—a performance of a new production of a Greek tragedy taking place at that very instant somewhere in Egypt, about a thousand miles away. We'll call it "distance viewing." Or, since we're Greek, maybe we'll call it "tele vision." Doesn't matter what we call it. In either case, folks will be able to see the play clearly, in Hi-Def, and observe every dance, hear every speech, watch all of the actor's facial expressions, the strumming of the lyre, the droning of the chorus, the sounds of the audience applauding, cheering, throwing roses on the stage, the whole thing. Not a simulation, not a reenactment, not a dramatization. The actual performance itself, as it's taking place. Faced with such a prediction, surely you—Aristotle—would raise your eyebrows, perhaps call in the Athenian equivalent of the men-in-white, have the fellow taken away, and then proceed with your studies of nature and the soul. Surely you would not, could not, take such a scenario seriously.

By the same token, no one could take the Santa scenario seriously. But at least we can say this: we know—albeit only very roughly—how the world would have to change in order for Santa to become possible. We know the type of work that would have to be accomplished, the type of discoveries that would have to be made. Not the work itself; not the discoveries themselves; for to know any of that would be already to have gone pretty far down the path toward actually accomplishing it. But we know the *kinds* of ways in which the world would have to change. We can't take seriously the prospect of those changes actually happening. Not even close. But nonetheless, we do have some idea of how different things in general would have to be for Santa, a single man with a handful of elves and a team of reindeer, to accomplish what today is accomplished, or at least approximated, by UPS, Federal Express, and the United States Postal Service combined, with all their trucks and airplanes and sorting machines and hundreds of thousands of employees. We can—barely—imagine that.

But try as we might, we cannot imagine any world in which justice has physical weight or in which love can be measured in feet and inches or in which pi tastes good. How could there be a world in which you can place justice on a scale and weigh it in ounces and pounds? Now—once again—let's not get all metaphorical! Yes, we do talk about justice and scales all the time. "The scales of justice." But I'm talking about the quality of justice itself—the fact that a decision is just or that a judge is the embodiment of justice or that the outcome of the game was just. And here, for such things, the concept of physical weight simply doesn't apply—any more than it applies to fairness or integrity or, switching gears yet again, to friendship or approval or egocentrism or majesty or honor or untold other things that are very, very important to us. It is impossible to imagine a world, any world, in which friendship can be weighed in ounces and pounds like an apple—or like an astronaut in space.

Perhaps we can imagine a world in which friendly people—people who enjoy friendship—are heavier than other people. So perhaps we could put all kinds of people on scales and say of the heavy ones that they are manifestations of friendship and of the skinny ones that they are manifestations of the absence of friendship. But an outward manifestation of a thing—the psychological or physical consequence of something—is not the same as the thing itself. Indeed, they're specifically different from the thing. Under the logic of cause and effect, the effect is explicitly something different from the cause. So when I'm talking about friendship—or justice or love, and so on—I'm talking about the thing itself. And in all such cases, it's simply impossible for us to imagine any world in which they could be weighed in ounces and pounds. To have the idea of such a world would require the concept of justice having physical weight, and there is not, and can never be, any such concept.

In roughly the same way, there is not, and can never be, a concept of God. We can never have the idea of a world that didn't have a beginning. Something must have started everything—a First Thing, an Unmoved Mover. Given the logic of cause and effect under which we operate, we are forced to think that there was an original cause. But we can also never have the idea of an original cause. For if there was an original cause, then that cause must have existed; and given the logic of cause and effect under which all of us operate, we are forced to think that everything that has existed was caused by something external to itself that was already in existence—as a result of which the original cause must itself have been caused, hence cannot have been the original cause, and so on ad infinitum.

The concept of God, if there were such a concept, would be the concept of something that must absolutely have existed and that—equally—cannot possibly have existed. There is simply no such concept. Our minds cannot entertain such an idea. We cannot have the idea of something that both exists and doesn't exist at the same time.

Moreover, we cannot imagine—we cannot have the idea of—a world in which this could be possible. What would such a world look like? What would have to change in order for something both to be and not to be? We have, and can have, no such idea. I can imagine a world in which I can dunk a basketball. I can even imagine a world in which Santa does his thing. But just as I can't imagine a world in which triangles have either more or less than 180 degrees or in which friendship weighs a quarter of a pound like a hunk of baloney, so I can't imagine—can't have the idea of—a world in which some particular thing does and must exist and, equally, does not and cannot exist. There is no such idea, and no idea of a world in which there could be such an idea.

There are, of course, many different kinds of Conceptual Impossibility. So far I've only scratched the surface. Take another example: it's impossible to have the concept of a married bachelor. A bachelor is by definition unmarried. If he's married, he's not a bachelor, and if he's a bachelor, he's unmarried. Here, then, is a classic case of a basic rule of thought: nothing can be X and non-X at the same time. George cannot be both married and unmarried at the same time. There's no such concept. It's Conceptually Impossible. In the same way, Emily cannot be both pregnant and not pregnant at the same time; Abe Lincoln cannot be both (physically) dead and (physically) alive at the same time.

Now in a certain sense God seems to be rather like this: something that both must exist (X) and cannot possibly exist (non-X) at the same time. A contradiction. But in fact, the case of God is really much worse than that. If you say that George is a married bachelor, we simply point out that he can't be both. He must be either married or a bachelor. And then, of course, we find out if George has a wife. If he does, he's married; if he doesn't, he's a bachelor. Either way, problem solved. With George, in other words, we're free to discover which is correct: bachelor or married. The trouble with God, on the other hand, is that we don't have such an option. God absolutely *must* exist and absolutely *cannot* exist at the same time. We're not free to discover which it is. It must be both. Under the logic of cause and effect, God—or something like God—must have started the world, since the world must have started somehow, and yet cannot have started the world, since whatever started the world must itself have come from somewhere or something. Of course, all of that is Conceptually Impossible. But here, unlike the case of George, there's no way out. If you say that George is a married bachelor, you've essentially made a mistake, a correctable mistake. He's either one or the other. But if you're talking about God, there's no simple "one-or-the-other" option. You can't say: okay then, God must exist, case closed. And you also can't simply say: okay, God cannot exist, case closed. It has to be both—which is Conceptually Impossible.

That's in part why I rather like the cases of the triangle and the weight-in-ounces-and-pounds of justice. They seem to capture the sense of deep, utter, eternal and irreversible impossibility.[3] But even here, the case of God is different. After all, it's not absolutely necessary that we find a triangle having internal angles either more or less than 180 degrees; it's not absolutely necessary that we discover the weight of justice in ounces and pounds. But with God, it's absolutely necessary both that the Unmoved Mover exists and that the Unmoved Mover cannot possibly exist. In this respect, the Conceptual Impossibility of God may be a unique kind of Conceptual Impossibility. It is, I suspect, sui generis. There's nothing quite like it. It is, one might say, the impossibility to end all impossibilities.

And so with respect to God, I am *aproleptic*. That's what I am. A convinced, committed, dyed-in-the wool, card-carrying aproleptic, through and through.

You should know, by the way, that I just made up that word. Aproleptic. At least I think I made it up. I myself have certainly never seen it before. The other day I googled it. Nothing. In any case, the doctrine I'm proposing in this book needs to have a name, so I'm going to call it *aprolepticism*. I'm neither a theist nor an atheist nor an agnostic. I am an aproleptic, an apostle of aprolepticism.

And just how did I come up with that name? Well, there's a word out there, a real word, which is *prolepsis*—a three-dollar term if there ever was one. It actually has a number of different meanings, but according to one of those meanings—derived from the ancient philosopher Epicurus—a prolepsis is a concept of something, pretty much anything, and a concept, moreover, that one already has, before the fact. A prolepsis is a kind of preconception. Of course, I've been arguing with respect to God that there is no such concept at all, and there can never be such a concept. And so, following the Greek-based rule of the English language whereby the prefix "a" means "without," I'm arguing for aprolepticism. To be aproleptic is to understand and accept the utter Conceptual Impossibility of God. Since I understand and accept the utter Conceptual Impossibility of God, I'm aproleptic. And I'm suggesting that you should be too—if, that is, you want to make sense.

So what about the Exception Theory? You remember that one, from chapter 1. Yes, everything that exists has been caused to exist by something other than itself—*except* God. God's the exception. God's the one thing that escapes external causation. Causation is true of every existing thing other than God. But God is different. God exists but is not caused. God is the Unmoved Mover. The First Thing. We have the rule: everything that exists is caused. But God is the exception—the exception that, as we say lamely, proves the rule.

I think we're now in a position to see why this won't work.

The problem is that the concept of existing—the very idea of something being in existence—includes within it the idea that it was caused by something other than itself. *That's just what it means to exist.* Underscore. Italics. Emphasis. That's an essential part of the idea of existence. To exist *means* (in part) to have been caused by something else. The logic of cause and effect simply doesn't allow for exceptions. There is no idea there.

Here's an SAT-type analogy: existence is to causation as triangle is to internal angles of 180 degrees. Let me run that by you again, because it's really important: existence is to causation as triangle is to internal angles of 180 degrees. The idea of a triangle is (in part) that it has internal angles of 180 degrees, no more, no less. If it doesn't have internal angles of 180 degrees, it's not a triangle. Anything else is Conceptually Impossible. Having internal angles of 180 degrees is an essential aspect of what makes a triangle a triangle.

It's part of the meaning of triangle. A triangle having internal angles of more or less than 180 degrees is a thought that we can't have. There is no such thought. In other words, no exceptions. An exception is literally unthinkable. What would an exception be? How would it look? How would we even begin to think about it, much less draw it? We couldn't. There's no idea there.

And so too for existence and causation. The idea of existence *requires* a cause. Remember, under the logic of cause and effect within which we all operate, no thing can come from nothing. Existing things—not just every known existing thing but the *very idea* of something, anything, existing—must have been caused to exist by something other than themselves. That's part of what it means to exist. Just as we can't dream up a triangle—not even an exceptional one—having internal angles of more or less than 180 degrees, so we can't dream up something existing that wasn't caused to exist by something other than itself. It's a thought—it's a dream—that we can't have. No exceptions.

It's impossible to say that all bachelors are unmarried except for one. Actually, that's false. We can say it. We can utter a grammatically correct sentence. We can say: "There exists a married bachelor." But the fact that we can utter those words doesn't mean that we're saying anything intelligible. And in fact we're not. "There's George over there. He's our exception. He's a bachelor, and a happily married one at that." Which is incoherent, irrational, unthinkable, impossible. It's gibberish. Noise. Gobbledygook. Conceptually Impossible.

Just as there can be no exceptions to the rule about bachelors being unmarried, because anything else is Conceptually Impossible; just as there can be no exceptions to the rule about triangles having internal angles of 180 degrees, because anything else is Conceptually Impossible; so too is it impossible—Conceptually Impossible—for there to be something that exists that wasn't caused to exist by something other than itself. There's no idea there.

So let's say we have God, and he's up there in heaven, in the misty firmament, wearing his flowing robes, all silk and satin and gauzy fabric, sitting on the throne, with long white hair and a long gray beard, looking for all the world like a cross between Karl Marx and the Dude, surrounded by all the wonderful stuff that's in heaven, the beautiful landscaping, the flowers and the harps, the whitewashed balustrades and the weeping willows, which are, of course, weeping for joy, and the angels, the gentle breezes, the shafts of luminous sunshine, and he's doing his thing, creating universes and destroying universes, a flood here, an earthquake there, you know, just doing all the things God does. There he is. God. And yet, nonetheless, despite our best efforts, we're still forced, absolutely forced, to ask: Where did he come from in the first place? Because if he exists, something must have caused him to exist. That's what the logic of cause and effect requires us to think. So we're forced to ask questions. Where are his mommy and daddy? Or where are the spirits or magical chemicals or higher powers that brought him into being? What Super-God created God? And then, what Super-Super-God created the Super-God that created God? And so on. Under the logic of cause and effect, the concept of something—anything—existing requires that thing to have an origin in something other than itself. And of course, that origin must itself have existed, in which case it must have been caused to exist by something other than itself, and so on and so on, ad infinitum.

There really can't have been a First Thing, an Unmoved Mover, God. The concept of existence—our concept of existence, just like our concept of triangle or our concept of bachelor—simply doesn't allow it. But if there wasn't a First Thing, then how did everything get started? Under the logic of cause and effect, something must have started everything. So there must have been a First Thing. But—here we go yet again—there cannot have been a First Thing, since if it existed, then something must have caused *it* to exist. And—well, by now you know the drill.

A few pages ago, we saw how the case of God is different from the other cases, like the case of the triangle, for instance. The impossibility of God is, we said, sui generis. I think that made sense. But now we're in an even better position to understand exactly why.

In effect, the (so-called) idea of God is hit with a double whammy. We've seen the first whammy. There can be no idea of an Unmoved Mover since, under the logic of cause and effect within which we all operate, everything that exists must have been caused by something other than itself. That's Whammy One. But at the same time it's absolutely necessary that there *was* an Unmoved Mover, since something must have started the world. The world cannot have come from just nothing and nowhere. So there cannot have been, but at the same time must have been, an Unmoved Mover. And of course, that's impossible. It's impossible—Conceptually Impossible—to have the idea of something that necessarily exists and cannot possibly exist at the same time. Nothing can be both what it is and what isn't at the same time. To think otherwise is to think gibberish, gobbledygook. No such idea.

And there is the second whammy—Whammy Two—and a heck of a whammy it is. Whammy Two says that nothing can be what it is and what it isn't at the same time. So it's absolutely impossible for the Unmoved Mover to exist (Whammy One) and, at the same time, absolutely necessary that the Unmoved Mover exists (both of which, together, produce Whammy Two). Of course, Whammy One is no slouch. Indeed, one whammy—either of them—would be way more than enough to kill the idea of God all by itself. Two whammies is overkill. But two whammies there are. No way around it.

The idea of God—or, rather, the idea that there is an idea of God—is a loser on all sides. To talk about God is, and can only be, to talk nonsense. Noise. Balderdash. Or, to be more precise, balderdash dressed up in fancy clothes.

Mumbo-jumbo.

4

EVEN IF THE FLESH IS WILLING

Interestingly, some people have tried to use pretty much the same kind of argument that I've been making in order to make pretty much the opposite point. They claim that my kind of argument—with a couple of important twists here and there—actually proves the existence of God. These are true believers. Theists. They think the existence of God is demonstrable, and they claim that my argument—or something rather like it—provides the demonstration.

Take, for example, Samuel Clarke. There are, I suppose, thousands of Sam Clarkes out there, but the one I'm talking about is the Reverend Samuel Clarke, an important English thinker of the late seventeenth and early eighteenth century. The Reverend Clarke was a so-called rationalist philosopher. He was also a guy who really got around. Among many other things, he was pals with Isaac Newton and a strong early supporter of Newton's science. Perhaps equally impressive, he was a pretty good friend of none other than the Queen of England herself. Eventually, he became the Rector of St. James of Westminster—an important position in Anglican circles—and was very much interested in proving the existence of God.

I think Clarke would accept almost everything I've said so far. Every effect must be preceded in time by a cause. This means there must have been an Unmoved Mover, something that started it all, something that got the world going in the first place. But if the Unmoved Mover existed, then it must have been caused as well, in which case it wasn't really the Unmoved Mover at all but, rather, the effect of a previous cause, which in turn was the effect of a previous cause, and so on ad infinitum. All of which presents serious difficulties, as I've described.

Clarke's solution? The Unmoved Mover—God—exists and must have existed, since, again, something must have started everything. The logic of cause and effect requires a beginning. But if God exists—if God is the beginning—then God must be spirit. Not matter, but spirit. That's Clarke's proposition. God is not a hunk of stuff like you and me. God is not a material entity composed of atoms and elements and molecules. God is not something to be seen, touched, heard, smelled, tasted. God doesn't have a physical shape or form. God is not a thing. To the contrary: God is spirit. God is immaterial. God is insubstantial. And what this means is that God didn't have to be caused by anything else. An Unmoved Mover.

According to Clarke, the logic of cause and effect is a logic of material things causing other material things. But if God is spirit—not a material thing—then we solve the problem. God-the-spirit caused the world. But since God-the-spirit is not matter, He (She? It?) was not caused. If the logic of cause and effect only applies to material things, says Samuel Clarke, we get out of the trap if we say that God is spirit, not matter.

Now there are all kinds of difficulties with this. Part of the problem is that spirit-talk is always hard to pin down, and that's because spirit is one of those amazing words in the English language that can mean all kinds of very different things. Of course, a spirit is a ghost—which opens up a whole can of worms in its own right. After all, sometimes ghosts are holy, as in Trinitarian versions of Christianity—the Father, the Son, and the Holy Spirit—and sometimes they're just plain old ordinary ghosts, like George and Marion, who became best friends with Cosmo Topper. (And if you remember *Topper*, either the original 1937 movie version or the 1953 TV sitcom, you're showing your age.) A lot of ghosts are spooky. But Casper was an extremely friendly ghost. Sometimes, of course, a spirit is not a ghost at all but an angel. And sometimes it's a demon. Sometimes it's a fairy, sometimes it's a sprite. Tinker Bell was a spirit—and, as imagined by Walt Disney, here was a spirit that looked less like Casper and more like a prototype for Barbie.

But of course, there's a great deal more to be said. After all, a spirit is a soul. I'm talking, for example, about your soul—as distinguished from your body. A spirit is also an animating principle, or a defining principle, or an essential principle. For example, there's the spirit of the law (see the great book of the same name by Baron de Montesquieu), or the Spirit of '76—which might refer to a heroic revolution or a place where you fill it up with unleaded. A spirit can be a mood, a feeling, an emotion: Ed was in lousy spirits, but Trixie was in quite good spirits. It can be an attitude: the Spartans at Thermopylae put up a spirited defense against the invading Persians. Spirit can be a feeling of loyalty and devotion as, for example, when the Mariners players have a lot of team spirit. Or it can be a simple matter of enthusiasm, as in certain parts of California where the cheerleaders are called the Spirit Squad. And if the Latin origins of the word *spirit* have something to do with breathing, modern usage often pertains less to gasses inhaled than to liquids imbibed. Of course, some spirits will kill you pretty quickly if you drink them—mineral spirits, spirits of ammonia. But others will only get you pleasantly high, though if you drink too much of them they can kill you just as well.

Now presumably when Samuel Clarke is talking about God-as-spirit, he's not talking about a fifth of Grey Goose. But what is he talking about? What kind of thing is a spiritual thing? What's the evidence for the existence of such things? What does it mean for them to exist? And do we really want to buy into a peculiar, occult world of ghosts and sprites, of angels and demons, of séances and voodoo, of fairy tales and overwrought imaginings? Are we really willing to accept all of that? Isn't that the very epitome of mumbo-jumbo?

So this is troubling. But in fact, the trouble goes deeper, much deeper.

To begin with, it's not clear how a spiritual thing—if such a thing existed—could cause a material thing to exist. Indeed, it's unclear how a spiritual thing could have any kind of impact on a material thing. How could a purely spiritual entity cause a material entity to move in any way at all?

Under the logic of cause and effect, it's pretty easy for us to imagine how one material thing can have a causal impact on another material thing. A spherical hunk of matter composed of rubber and string and rawhide—let's call it a baseball—is hurtling through the air. About sixty feet and six inches away, a long, cylindrical hunk of matter composed of wood—let's call it a bat—is waiting, presumably in somebody's hands, maybe someone like Barry Bonds. As the baseball approaches, the bat swings and makes contact with the baseball, and the baseball suddenly rockets in a different direction. Our ordinary consciousness has no great difficulty imagining what happens when one material object hits or otherwise makes physical contact with another material object. Something, some material thing, causes some other thing, another material thing, to move. That, in a nutshell, is the logic of cause and effect. That, according to our ordinary way of thinking, is pretty much how the world works. Atoms collide with atoms, molecules with molecules, baseballs with bats. But how could a spiritual thing—something that's not material at all—hit or physically engage or otherwise move a material thing?

Imagine, for example, an absolutely perfect vacuum. A vacuum is something that contains nothing—no atoms, no elements, no molecules, no subatomic particles. Imagine, in other words, the perfect absence of anything material. Utter emptiness. It's hard to see how a vacuum could hit anything. There'd be nothing to do the hitting. It would be like trying to hit a baseball without a bat and without anything else to replace the bat. It would be like trying to hit a baseball with air. Except, of course, it would be even worse than that, since air is not spirit and not even a vacuum but is composed of lots of material things, atoms and molecules and other very tiny bits of stuff. So it would be like trying to hit a baseball with "air" from which all atoms and molecules have been removed. It's hard, no impossible, for the ordinary mind to imagine something completely immaterial having a causal effect on—moving—something physical. It seems to be Conceptually Impossible.

This is such a serious problem that one of Samuel Clarke's successors, George Berkeley, decided we had to think about the world in a completely different way. Now Berkeley was a great philosopher of the eighteenth century—far more important than Clarke. He was also an Anglican bishop who, like any good bishop, was committed to the existence of God. A true believer. Like Clarke, he believed that God must be entirely spirit. But he couldn't figure out how God-as-spirit could have any kind of causal interaction with material things—just like you and I can't figure out how a vacuum could hit a baseball.[1] Conceptually Impossible. So Berkeley came up with a nifty solution. If we have trouble understanding how God-the-spirit could have a causal impact on material things, then let's not give up on the existence of God. Instead, let's give up on the existence of material things. And that's exactly what Berkeley did. There are, he said, no material things at all. Matter simply does not exist. There are no baseballs, no bats. No atoms, no molecules. There are no bodies. No flesh, no blood, no bones. You don't have a body, and neither do I. No cars, no boats. No mountains to be climbed, no rivers to be crossed. No rocks, no flowers, no kitty-cats, no grizzly bears. No bread, no butter, no jam. The only things that exist are ideas. Instead of a baseball, there's only the idea of a baseball; instead of a bat, the idea of a bat. And so on. That, says Berkeley, solves the problem. The world exists entirely as a series of immaterial ideas in our minds. It is, so to speak, just a figment of our imagination. Since we can understand how one idea can cause—or, rather, lead to—another idea (the idea of three, the idea of five, and the idea of addition, all taken together, lead to the idea of eight), we have no trouble understanding how God-the-spirit caused the world. God is a mind. As such, God has ideas. God's ideas lead to other ideas, like the idea of a bat and the idea of a baseball. You and I are also minds—not bodies, not flesh and bone, just minds. So we have ideas, including ideas of a bat and a baseball and lots of others. We get our ideas from God. Presto. No more contradiction. And oh, by the way, God exists.

If you think this argument is preposterous, you should know, first of all, that Bishop Berkeley made it with great ingenuity. He was an extraordinary thinker, and the argument isn't quite as ridiculous as it might seem. Not quite. In fact, you should also know that it's possible, just possible, that the argument actually works in some sense—by which I mean it's possible that it's a philosophically coherent argument, an argument that can be made to satisfy the standards of formal logical rigor. Most philosophers doubt this, and so do I. But the jury's still out, and to this day Berkeley has his defenders. But finally, you should know what I suspect you already know, namely, that Berkeley's position is deeply out of line with what ordinary folk, you and I, are able to believe and understand, deep down. Interestingly, Berkeley himself denies this. He thinks his view is, in fact, the commonsense view. And really, who am I to argue? Berkeley was truly a certifiable genius. Nonetheless, I don't get it. I don't think it works, at least not for you and me. But here's the bottom line: if you really want to believe that the baseball flying through the gap in left-center field after it was hit by a mighty swing of the bat is simply a figment of your imagination, just an idea; if you want to believe that the birthday cake you're eating, with all of its sweetness and chocolate goodness, is not really a cake at all but the mere thought of a cake; if you want to believe that Aunt Minnie—who gave birth to your cousins and who took care of you when your mom was sick and who made wonderful spaghetti and who tragically died after a courageous bout with cancer—if you want to believe that she never really existed except as an idea; if you want to deny that the Holocaust really occurred except as a thought or series of thoughts, so that there weren't really any gas chambers and cattle cars and torture and other horrible things—if you want to believe things like this, well, you go right ahead. But I'd suggest that your beliefs would be way, way out of whack with ordinary consciousness, including your own real, deep-down beliefs.

And remember, that's what this book, the book you're now reading, is all about—trying to discover what our own beliefs are and to figure out how we should think about things, including God, in a way that makes sense to us.

If somehow we were able to solve this first problem—the conceptual problem of God-as-spirit having a causal impact on physical things—we'd still have trouble trying to determine just how such a God could have made material things. Under the logic of cause and effect—hence from the perspective of ordinary thought—it's hard to imagine this happening. Even if the first material thing that existed was a tiny atom, or an even smaller subatomic particle, we still have to ask how God-as-spirit could have caused that tiny thing to come into existence.

Specifically, we'd have to ask: out of what was that first atom or subatomic particle made? What did God-as-spirit use to make it? What were the raw materials? Of course, if there were raw materials out of which God-as-spirit made the first atom or subatomic particle, then that atom or subatomic particle was not the First Physical Thing. The raw material was the First Physical Thing. But then, where did *that* come from? And so on, ad infinitum. So if God-as-spirit made the first atom or subatomic particle but didn't make it out of any raw materials, what did He make it out of? Did He (She? It?) make it out of nothing? According to our ordinary consciousness—according to the logic of cause and effect—that just can't be. No physical thing can come out of nothing. Even Samuel Clarke agrees with that. But this puts Clarke in a bind. Clarke goes for the idea of God-as-spirit because he agrees that physical things are governed by the logic of cause and effect, meaning that all physical things are causes of, and also effects of, other physical things. That's the reason he thinks God must be spirit. It—spirit—is outside of the logic of cause and effect. But if physical things, though not spiritual things, are governed by the logic of cause and effect, then the first atom or subatomic particle—a physical thing—must be equally so governed. The first physical thing must have been the physical cause of the second physical thing; but since it's a physical thing, it too must have been caused by some other physical thing—in which case, it wasn't the First Physical Thing at all. It looks like, on Clarke's own account, the First Physical Thing must have been crafted by God-as-spirit out of some other physical thing, in which case we're back to our original problem.

Either God-as-spirit created the first atom or subatomic particle out of some raw material, in which case we have to ask where the raw material came from, meaning that it must have come from some previous raw material, and so on ad infinitum; or else God-as-spirit created the first atom or subatomic particle literally out of nothing, which is a problem for Clarke, since he believes that physical entities, though not spiritual entities, are governed by the logic of cause and effect. It's also a problem for us since our ordinary way of thinking requires us to believe that no thing can come out of nothing.

But even if we could somehow work our way through all this, a fundamental question would remain: why is the logic of cause and effect limited to physical things?

Suppose we posit the existence of spiritual things: ghosts and goblins and God-as-spirit. It's just not clear how this would help. Because if we posit the existence of those kinds of things, we're saying that, well, they do indeed exist. But then we have to ask: if they exist, where did they come from? You want to say that spirits exist?

Fine. But the logic of cause and effect under which we operate still requires us to wonder what caused them to exist? Maybe the cause wasn't physical. Maybe it was spiritual—whatever that might mean. But the logic remains. Whatever exists must have come from somewhere. No thing—physical or otherwise—can come from nothing. Literally the absence of anything and everything, physical or spiritual, cannot, according to our lights, produce anything. Things are produced by other things. That's how things get to be things. And it doesn't seem to matter if the thing is physical or not. If it exists, something must have brought it about. And whatever brought it about must also have existed. And since it existed, something must have brought it about in turn. And so on, ad infinitum.

So the notion of God-as-spirit doesn't really help one bit. Actually, this was pointed out in the eighteenth century, not that long after Samuel Clarke proposed his theory, by another British philosopher—in fact the greatest of all British philosophers—David Hume.[2] It was Hume who said Clarke didn't go back far enough. If we want to know what caused the world and we say that the answer is God, this still begs the question: where did God come from? If Clarke really believes that no thing can come from nothing (something that Hume by the way actually doubted), then Clarke has to go all the way with this and ask about the origin(s) of God. Which, of course, gets us right back where we started, namely, with the idea of something that absolutely must exist and cannot possibly exist—which is not an idea at all.

So all this is an argument for atheism, right?

No. Actually, it's not.

5

ATHEISM . . .

The atheist believes—or, rather, claims to believe—that God doesn't exist.[1] But God has to exist. Remember, under the logic of cause and effect, the world, if it exists, must have had a cause. After all, everything that exists was necessarily caused by something other than itself whose existence preceded it, and applies to the world as much as to anything, since the world exists.[2] What could it possibly mean to say that the world exists but it never got started? So the existence of the world absolutely requires that there was a First Cause—an Unmoved Mover, God—that caused the world to exist in the first place. In a sense, we cannot *not* believe in God. Atheism is simply unavailable to us. No one in his right mind can truly be an atheist.

Of course, the belief in God—theism—is equally unavailable to us. Because if God did exist—a First Cause or an Unmoved Mover—then under the logic of cause and effect something or someone must have caused *it* to exist. And if something caused *it* to exist, then it cannot have been the First Cause or Unmoved Mover or God. The thing that caused it came first; but of course, *that* thing must itself have been caused by something else; and so on, ad infinitum. So God simply cannot exist. The impossibility of atheism is matched by the impossibility of theism.

Now you can certainly *say* you're an atheist. You can utter words to that effect, and you can do so in complete, grammatically correct sentences. By the same token, as we've seen, my friend can say he believes the Mariners will win the pennant. He can utter the words in a way that satisfies the rules of grammar. But if he thinks about it a while, he'll realize he doesn't actually believe it at all. And so too for atheists—and for theists as well.

To talk about God is to talk about something that cannot possibly exist and, at the same time, absolutely must exist. But we cannot have the idea of something that both exists and doesn't exist at the same. There's no such concept. So to ask if that concept, which is not a concept at all, describes anything in the world, or even anything that could be in the world, is to ask a non-question. There's no concept about which to ask. If we want to ask about the existence of Nessie or of Santa or of me dunking, that's completely different. In those cases, we know what we're talking about, because we have concepts—the concept of Nessie or the concept of Santa or the concept of me dunking. If I ask you whether or not you believe in Santa, I'm asking a real question and you can provide a real answer. But in the case of God—no can do. Since atheism and theism both purport to be answers to the question of the existence of God, and since there is no such question, atheism and theism are both—and equally—impossible.

Actually, there's a second reason to reject atheism—or rather, a second and more extended version of the same argument. Now this is going to get a little tricky, maybe more tricky than it needs to be. But if you have any lingering doubts about the impossibility of atheism—and my hunch is that you do—the argument is important.

Suppose I tell you that I don't believe in the existence, actual or possible, of ghroblingats. Specifically, I claim that there are no ghroblingats now, there never have been any, and there never will be any. They are impossible. With respect to ghroblingats, I'm a complete non-believer. I am to ghroblingats as atheists are to God—or, rather, as atheists claim they are to God.

Suppose, then, you ask me what is it about ghroblingats that suggests to me that they don't and can't exist? I respond that I don't know anything at all about ghroblingats. I just know that they don't exist.

"Well," you say, perplexed, "I myself have never heard of ghroblingats. What are they?"

I answer: "They're nothing."

"What do you mean they're nothing?"

"I mean that I just made up the word. Right now. I thought of a silly word. It's just a word, a new word. It has no meaning. Since it has no meaning, it's really not even a word. It's a noise that I just made up. Ghroblingats. Kind of a neat sound, isn't it?"

"You just made up?"

"Just like that."

Now you're irritated: "What do you mean it has no meaning?"

"When I say that it has no meaning, I'm saying that it doesn't denote anything. There's no concept—no idea—of a ghroblingat. I wasn't thinking of any particular thing—no object, no image, no entity, no relationship, no idea, no value, no characteristic, no fantasy, no trait, no attitude, no symbol, no feeling. I had—and have—no idea of a ghroblingat. There is no concept. It's just a noise that I made up and then spelled out, more or less phonetically, so that it sounds like and looks like a word, even though it isn't one."

"So you say that ghroblingats don't exist?"

"How could they?" I respond. "I just made them up."

At which point, you look me in the eye, frown, and slowly stroke your chin: "What are the 'they' and the 'them' that you're talking about when you say 'they don't exist' and when you say you 'just made them up'? If there's no concept, then what are 'they'? What kinds of things would they be if they existed? To what kinds of things does the 'they' and the 'them' refer?"

After mulling that over, I'm forced to respond: "I don't know how to answer that question."

You continue: "So what would it mean for ghroblingats to exist? Can you tell me that?"

I can't.

Actually, my preference would be to respond to your question by saying that ghroblingats would exist if something with all the traits of a ghroblingat existed. But that can't be right, since ghroblingats have no traits. There's no concept of a ghroblingat.

The concept of a thing—any particular thing—is largely an account of what that thing is; and an account of the thing is usually a list and description of the characteristics or features or elements or traits or component parts or structure of the thing. (Actually, many philosophers would not say that exactly, but don't worry about it. For present purposes this will work just fine.) So the concept is in part what identifies the thing as the kind of thing it is and in part what distinguishes it from other particular things. The concept of Santa is essentially composed of the white beard and the red suit and the belly that shakes like a bowl full of jelly and the reindeer and the "ho, ho, ho" and so on. The concept of me is, well, the characteristics that make me who I am and that distinguish me from everyone else. The concept of me dunking a basketball includes the concept of me plus all of those things—the ball, the hoop, the floor, the jump—that make dunking what it is. But the concept of a ghroblingat includes no characteristics or features or elements. Hence, the very phrase "the concept of a ghroblingat" is a mistake. There is no concept. It's just a nonsensical utterance. It doesn't denote anything.

Of course, the utterance itself exists—as an utterance. The noise, the pure physical sound, that comes out of my mouth—the sound "ghroblingat"—now that exists. But that noise, in and of itself, has no meaning.[3] It's just noise. It doesn't express a concept. As such, it doesn't point to anything that could exist; nor, however, does it point to anything that couldn't exist. It doesn't point.

That's important because it shows that ghroblingats are—in these respects—very different from, for example, Santa. Now, we all know that none of us believes in Santa. But notice: we don't believe in *him*. We don't believe in the existence of the thing that the concept "Santa" points to or describes. Which means that we know what it is—we have an idea of what it is—that we don't believe in. We have a concept of the thing that we can refer to when we say we don't believe that it describes anything that can exist. In fact, it's precisely because I know what the concept of Santa is that I also know that he's Physically Impossible. Similarly, I don't believe that I could dunk. I don't believe in *it*. I don't believe in the possible existence of the thing that the concept "Peter dunking" describes. Again, I know what it is—I have an idea of what it is—that I believe to be impossible; and again, the impossibility makes sense only because I have the concept of the thing itself. Of course, and as a direct result of all this, I know a lot of other things besides. In the cases of Santa and me dunking, for example, I have a pretty good idea of what the existence of the thing, if it had been possible, would have entailed. In each such case, I have some sense of how the world would have to change in order to accommodate the existence of what I believe to be impossible. In each such case, I can imagine at least roughly what it would look like for such a thing to exist. And in each case, I have at least some strong notion as to what it is that makes the existence of the thing impossible.

But with ghroblingats, I have none of that. I neither believe nor disbelieve in the existence of ghroblingats, since I literally don't know what I'm talking about. Indeed, I'm not talking about anything. There is no concept. There is nothing—no idea—to which I'm referring. And I really don't have the slightest inkling of what it could mean to think about the existence of something that the concept ghroblingat describes—for the very simple reason that it's not a concept at all, hence describes nothing. Nor could I think about the non-existence of ghroblingats, and for the very same reason. There is *no* "it" the existence or non-existence of which comes into question.

I have no idea what the existence of ghroblingats would entail. I wouldn't know how to begin thinking about that. I have no sense of how the world would have to change to accommodate ghroblingats. Again, I wouldn't know how to begin thinking about that. I certainly cannot imagine what it would look like for such a thing to exist. Without a concept, there's nothing to imagine. The word *ghroblingats*—which is not really a word—has no reference, neither concrete nor abstract. It is pure gibberish, gobbledygook, nonsense, without any content at all. And so, the question of ghroblingats existing—possibly or actually—doesn't arise. There is nothing the existence or non-existence of which to discuss. There's nothing to talk about, nothing to think about, nothing to which one might refer.

It is, I believe, pretty much the same with the idea of a triangle whose internal angles add up to either more or less than 180 degrees. There is no such idea, and therefore the existence of something in the world that's an example or approximation of that idea just doesn't arise. I cannot say that such a thing either exists or doesn't since there's literally nothing to talk about. If there's no idea, then there's nothing to discuss—including the question of something either existing or not existing to which that idea, of which there is none, applies.

Now what I've just said about triangles is probably flat-out wrong. Or rather, what I've said is right only if we accept Euclidean premises—for example, the premise that parallel lines never intersect. But few if any physicists today believe that the world itself—the real world out there—satisfies Euclidean premises. Space, they now tell us, may well be intrinsically curved (especially at the "local" level, if not on the very largest scale). This means, among many other things, that seemingly parallel lines will eventually intersect—they are actually curved—and that it's possible, indeed easy, for a triangle to have internal angles other than 180 degrees. So the triangle example is really a lousy example.

But bear with me. Suppose that we were operating within Euclidean premises. Just suppose. What, then, would a triangle with internal angles of either less or more than 180 degrees look like? How would we draw it? What is the "it" that you'd be attempting to draw? What would its characteristics be?

There are no conceivable answers. There are no conceivable answers because there's no such idea.

But doesn't that just prove that it's impossible, under Euclidean premises, to create an object that approximates a triangle with internal angles either less or more than 180 degrees? Isn't that a coherent thing to say? Haven't I just demonstrated the impossibility of such a thing ever existing?

Well, not really. Think about it. You take a pencil and piece of paper and—working within Euclidean premises—you sit down to draw (an approximation of) a triangle with internal angles either more or less than 180 degrees. Let's say, for the sake of argument, 200 degrees. That's what you're trying to do: draw a triangle having internal angles of 200 degrees. Now always remember, you're not trying to draw (an approximation of) a triangle with internal angles of exactly 180 degrees. You're not trying to draw a plain old triangle. Anyone can do that. If you want to do that, no problem. You just sit down with pencil and paper, and also with the idea of a plain old triangle in your head, and then you use that idea to guide your drawing. Or, looked at the other way around, your drawing is an effort to create a material approximation—an instantiation, as philosophers sometimes say—of the idea. If you did that, you'd almost certainly succeed. Anyone can draw a plain old triangle, at least roughly. But that's *not* what I'm now asking you to do. I'm asking you, Euclidean that you are, to draw (an approximation of) a triangle—a three-sided polygon formed by connecting three points not in a straight line by straight-line segments—that has internal angles of 200 degrees. Now picture this. You're sitting there. You're ready to go, ready to draw. You've got pencil and paper but—no idea. No concept. No thought. There's nothing for you to do. Where would you start? How would you proceed? And let's be clear: you can't do this—you can't try to draw a triangle having 200 degrees—by trying to draw a plain old triangle, since that means drawing (an approximation of) a triangle with internal angles of exactly 180 degrees. That's not the task. So then, what? What do you do? How do you begin? If, somehow, you managed to draw a line, what's the second thing you'd draw?

Basically, I think you'd be paralyzed. I think your hand couldn't move, since you'd have no idea where or how to move it. And to say that it's therefore impossible to draw (an approximation of) a triangle with internal angles of 200 degrees doesn't really get at what's going on. The task is not impossible. It's literally inconceivable. Unable to move my pencil, I wouldn't have failed at the task. I really wouldn't know what the task is. There is no task, nothing at which to fail.

Notice how this is completely different from the task of trying to draw an absolutely perfect plain old triangle—a triangle having exactly 180 degrees. That's impossible too, since anything we draw would probably be at least microscopically inaccurate (which means that it wouldn't actually be a triangle). But at least here we know exactly what we're trying to do. We know what it means. We have an idea. It's Physically Impossible, but conceptually no problem at all.

From the perspective of Euclidean geometry, the phrase "a triangle having internal angles either more or less than 180 degrees" is really just noise—a mere sound, hardly different from ghroblingats. Well yes, it is different in this respect: unlike ghroblingats, the phrase does contain two entirely meaningful ideas, the idea of a triangle and the idea of something having internal angles more or less than 180 degrees. Nothing wrong with either of those ideas. But putting them together in an attempt to form a single concept—that produces little more than a meaningless grunt.

Now again, the triangle is a bad example, since we *can* in fact know how the world would have to change—or, rather, how we'd have to understand the world differently—in order for triangles not to have internal angles of 180 degrees. If space is curved—done. No problem.

So if it's such a bad example, why am I using it? Several reasons.

First, I really like the image of the Euclidean geometer sitting down to draw a triangle with internal angles of 200 degrees and just not knowing what to do. I think it's an effective image. I think—I hope—it illustrates just what it means when there's no concept. Again, it's not that we don't believe in the possible existence of the thing that the concept is supposed to describe. Rather, since there's no concept, the question of existence simply doesn't arise at all.

Second, while physicists say that space may be intrinsically curved, one has to ask—perhaps in all innocence and naïveté—are they actually right about this? I honestly don't know the answer, but I'm not convinced anyone does. To be brief: the fact that the math works out doesn't necessarily mean that it accurately describes what's happening in nature or that it provides ordinary humans with an understanding of how things in the world really are. Newton's math requires—posits—the force of gravity. Seems good. The apple falls off the tree and conks me on the head. Gravity, what else. But perhaps gravity is, in fact, simply something that's been—as we say—"posited." The alleged effects of gravity are observed every day, all the time. Apples are dropping from trees, constantly. But the thing itself—gravity itself, apart from all of the things that it's supposed to produce—eludes direct observation. We're told that it's a "force." We see what it does, but we've never actually seen it. So, arguably, we posit gravity because it helps the equations work out nicely, but that might be all it is—something that we've posited, invented, precisely *because* it makes the equations work. And indeed, there are, evidently, serious physicists today who deny the necessity—even the existence?—of gravity. Other things might be able to make the equations work just as well, perhaps even better. Similarly, Einstein's math assumes that space is intrinsically curved and that gravity is not so much a force as a manifestation of curvature. And indeed, given the intrinsic curvature of space, the mathematical analyses work out. But that doesn't necessarily mean they accurately describe how things in the world really are. Nor do they necessarily describe a world we can truly envision, imagine, and conceive. If, to pick a somewhat different and perhaps more graphic example, mathematicians can create a language that talks about more than three dimensions in space, does that mean ordinary humans can actually imagine—picture, conceptualize, comprehend, truly believe in the existence of—more than three dimensions? Not necessarily.

In this context, we also have to recall once again what this book is all about and what I'm trying to accomplish. Remember, the idea—the goal—is to discover what it is we really believe, despite what we sometimes say or sometimes think we believe. And by "we," I mean ordinary people—people like you and me. Now on several occasions I've explicitly ruled out insane people and small children. They don't think like we do. But perhaps there are others I should be explicitly ruling out as well. Perhaps I should be ruling out gurus or shamans. Perhaps I should be ruling out everyone who has had a lengthy, sit-down, face-to-face conversation with God. And perhaps I should be ruling out Albert Einstein and all the other top-flight physicists who, God bless 'em, might have no trouble at all envisioning, imagining, and conceiving—picturing, and then living in—a world vastly different from the world of ordinary experience. I have my doubts about all such people, but perhaps I'm ignorant—not having been a guru, not having had a chit-chat with the Almighty, and not having the slightest idea how to envision space having multiple dimensions. Indeed, I do plead ignorance. No false modesty there. Just the truth. But I'm not writing about any of that. I'm trying to figure out what's possible—what makes sense—for you and me, us plain folk, to think. Given how our minds work—and, in particular, given the logic of cause and effect—what should we believe? And, sorry to say, for poor humble souls like us, there is simply no concept of God, hence no way to ask, much less answer, the question of God's existence.

Poor humble souls like us must be—remember—aproleptic.

There is, however, one more reason why I'm sticking with the triangle example, and it's pretty important. For if non-Euclidean geometry is perfectly fine with the concept of a triangle having internal angles other than 180 degrees, there are plenty of other things that are, from a non-Euclidean perspective, not fine at all. With respect to geometry, Conceptual Impossibility is hardly the special province of the Euclidean mind. From the post-Einsteinian perspective, lots of things are Conceptually Impossible. The problem, however, is that explaining some of the things that are Conceptually Impossible for the non-Euclidean geometer would require a lot more math than most people have. Indeed, way more than I have! I myself am not good at math. Never was. Couldn't dunk a basketball, couldn't do math. To be sure, there are a few things that I do know. I do know, at least in the simplest case, how to find the derivative of a function. I have a rough sense of the astonishing relationship between the derivative and the integral. And I have a reasonable understanding of why it all matters, since much of what happens in the world—spaces and trajectories and economic performance and countless other things—may well be happening in curves, not straight lines. But don't push me much further than that. And I take it that at least some of you might not even know as much as I do. Now we could all, of course, get a whole lot better at math. And we should. That would be a good thing all around. But it would also take us pretty far afield, and for present purposes it wouldn't be worth it. It wouldn't be worth it mainly because the basic point would remain unchanged: the problems faced by the Euclidean geometer trying to draw a triangle having internal angles of either more or less than 180 degrees would be quite analogous to a range of problems that the non-Euclidean geometer would also have. In all such cases, Conceptual Impossibility would render the relevant question not unanswerable but essentially inexpressible. With respect to whether or not something exists, where there's no concept, there's no question.

But let's put triangles to rest, once and for all, and return to our other cases. How would you approach the task of weighing justice in ounces and pounds, or subjecting pi (remember, pi, not pie) to a taste test, or calculating the volume in cubic feet of friendship? Better examples, I think. These tasks are not impossible; they're unthinkable. They're unthinkable because the concepts involved are not really concepts at all. In each case, Conceptual Impossibility makes the question of the existence of the thing not impossible but completely and utterly unintelligible.

If you ask me whether or not I think ghroblingats exist, I really can't answer yes or no. The only thing I can say is "I don't know what you're talking about." You might as well ask me if bxgzgktl exists. To which my only plausible response would be "Huh?" I wouldn't understand what you're saying, because you wouldn't be saying anything intelligible. I can neither affirm nor deny the existence of bxgzgktl because that's just gibberish. There's no question to answer. There's nothing to affirm or deny. It's nonsense. And so too for ghroblingats. And for triangles having angles of either more or less than 180 degrees. And for the weight of justice in ounces and pounds.

And so too for God. Except that God is not just gibberish. It's mumbo-jumbo. Gibberish all gussied up. To talk about God is to talk about something that absolutely cannot exist and, at the same time, absolutely must exist. There is no such concept. From this, it follows neither that theism nor atheism is right but, to the contrary, neither can be right. Neither can be right because they are nothing other than answers to a question that is, in fact, not a question at all.

6

. . . AND AGNOSTICISM

Agnosticism won't work either.

Now, at first blush agnosticism seems to be a pretty reasonable way of looking at things. The agnostic simply says: we don't know. We don't have enough information—yet—to determine whether or not God exists. And without sufficient information, we simply can't decide. We're ignorant. Perhaps someday we'll figure it out. Perhaps someday the data will come our way. But for now—and for the foreseeable future—the question is, as we say, moot.

The agnostic thinks that theists are wrong—and worse. The trouble with theists is that they believe in God without sufficient evidence. They plan their lives, make fundamental decisions, sometimes pass laws or fight wars—all on the basis of nothing that could be called knowledge. This is, for the agnostic, bizarre and irresponsible. Before you fight a war, you ought to know what you're doing and why; and before you fight a war for God, you ought to be pretty darn sure that God exists. Evidence is crucial, and we don't have enough of it to believe in God. Not even close. But if agnostics are down on theists, they're also down on atheists. Atheists are convinced that God does not exist. Indeed, they often (though, as I've indicated, not always) claim to *know* that God doesn't exist. This is a belief that governs their lives and their actions. But again, it's based on nothing that could really be called knowledge. It's presumptuous, arrogant, uninformed. From the perspective of the agnostic, atheists are about as whacky as theists.

Since I also think both theism and atheism are wrong, I must be an agnostic, right? But in fact, no, not right. I believe agnosticism is wrong as well.

The problem with agnostics is that they think the question of the existence of God is an intelligible question. It's a question that makes sense. The claim that we don't—yet—have enough information doesn't mean it's a bad question. In fact, it means exactly and precisely the opposite. And that's a huge problem. You see, the agnostic's assertion that we don't have enough information to answer the question about God is itself an assertion that doesn't make any sense unless we believe the question to be perfectly intelligible. Think about it. It's only by understanding the question—understanding what it means—that we could decide we don't have enough evidence to answer it. So the problem isn't the question; the problem is information. If only we had enough information, we could answer the question—one way or the other.

I wake up in the morning and before looking out the window I wonder if it's raining. I don't know the answer, since I haven't yet looked out the window. I don't—yet—have enough information to answer the question. If my wife, who also hasn't looked out the window and anyway is trying to get back to sleep, asks me if it's raining, I have to tell her that I don't know. Before looking out the window, I'm agnostic on the question of whether or not it's raining. So in fact I do say to my wife: "Dear, I am, for the moment, agnostic on that question." Or words to that effect. But when I say that, I'm also saying that when I do look outside the window, I won't be agnostic any longer. I'll know the answer. This means, among other things, that I understand her question. It's a good question. It makes sense. When I look out the window I'll find out the answer, and then I'll let her know.

This is pretty much what the agnostic says when asked about the existence of God. I don't know—yet—but when I find out, I'll let you know. And again, this means that the agnostic understands the question. It's a good question.

For a question to be a good question, it has to be asking something that's intelligible. And this means it has to be asking about the existence of something that we have a concept of, something about which we have an idea. For if there's no concept—no idea—then all the evidence in the world would be useless. Indeed, evidence of—what?

You can't be agnostic with respect to the existence of ghroblingats. That would mean you're holding off until you get more evidence about them. But what kind of evidence would be relevant to the existence of ghroblingats? Again, evidence of what? How would the agnostic answer that question? Similarly, what kind of evidence would be relevant to questions about the weight of justice in ounces and pounds, or the taste of pi, or the cubic volume of friendship? Where would you begin to look? What kind of inquiry would you undertake? What kind of test would you invent?

But doesn't that just mean that ghroblingats don't exist, that justice has no weight, pi has no taste, friendship has no volume? Shouldn't the agnostic be "atheistic"—a non-believer—with respect to those things? Well, no. Those things are, indeed, Conceptually

Impossible. There are no thoughts there, no ideas. But precisely for that reason, to say that it's impossible for justice to have weight or for pi to be tasty or for friendship to have volume—this doesn't really get at what's going on. Because as I hope is clear by now, these things are not in the usual sense—the physical sense—impossible. They're literally inconceivable. They have no meaning. Unlike Santa, there's nothing there either to exist or not exist. There is no idea of the "they" about which to agree or disagree. Which means, in turn, that there's nothing about which to have evidence. In such cases, the very idea of evidence is absurd.

And so too for the existence of God. It's not that we don't have enough evidence. It's that there's no concept—no idea—about which we could gather evidence, one way or the other. We can never know about the existence or non-existence of God since—given the Conceptual Impossibility of God, i.e., of an Unmoved Mover that absolutely must exist and, at the same time, cannot possibly exist—there's literally nothing to know, one way or the other.

Clearly, then, both atheism and agnosticism are unsustainable. Neither of them makes any sense. But of the two, I think agnosticism is actually the worse. And in part that's precisely because it seems so reasonable. You see, I've been proposing that all of us have this underlying, hidden, implicit intuition. Despite what we sometimes say, we already know that in fact there's no concept of God. Deep down, that's what we really think. Deep down, we're all aproleptic. But for many of us, that's a worry. For many of us, it's kind of scary. The thought that God exists can be, well, awfully comforting, and so it's not easy for many of us to give it up, as a result of which we do everything we can to keep the skeleton—the aproleptic skeleton—locked up in the closet. But then the agnostic comes along and says: don't worry about any of it. Relax. Just hang in there. Chill. Sure, we don't have enough information. We don't know enough—yet—to prove the existence of God. But we also don't know enough to disprove it either. So let's just bide our time. Let's wait and see. No need to rush. Soon enough, we'll know what's up. And this gives us an excuse—a powerful excuse—to ignore our own deep-seated convictions. It prevents us from seeing the truth. It prevents us from coming to grips with our own inner convictions, the aproleptic within. And as we'll see, it actually prevents us from enjoying a kind of comfort—a kind of peace of mind—that's actually way more satisfying than anything we might get even from theism, much less from atheism or agnosticism.

All of which means that, in the last analysis, I'm going to have good news for you. In fact, wonderful news. But bear with me.

7

FULL FAITH AND NO CREDIT

All of which brings us back to faith.

One of the most important things to remember about faith is that you can never have just simply faith, all by itself. Faith always means faith *in* something, or faith *that* something exists or *that* something will happen. There's always something *about which* you have faith. But of course, this means that you can't have faith in something or about something unless you have at least some idea of what that "something" might be. You must have an idea of the thing in which you have faith.

So for example, you can certainly have faith in the existence of the Abominable Snowman, or of Bigfoot, or of Nessie. It's easy enough to have at least a rough idea of a sea monster swimming around in Loch Ness; and so if I say I believe in—I have faith in—the existence of Nessie, I know roughly what I'm talking about. In such a case, I would be believing in the existence of *that*. And if you were to ask me what the *that* is, I'd say: You know, that thing, the monster, swimming around over there in the lake in Scotland. Similarly, it's easy enough to have faith in my eventually being able to dunk a basketball. I know pretty much what that would mean, even if I have no idea how I'd get there. I think I can even have faith in the existence of Santa. Again, I know what it is that I'd be believing in—red suit, belly that shakes like a bowl full of jelly, and so on. In all such cases, faith is possible.

Of course, the fact that one *can* have faith in those things doesn't mean one *should*. I myself think it'd be silly—actually much worse than silly—to believe in the existence of Nessie, and I know it would be absurd to believe in my ability to dunk a basketball. Santa? Forget about it. But remember: that's an important part of faith. The more peculiar the belief, the better—at least from a faith-based point of view. If it's raining outside and I see for myself that it's raining outside, I don't have faith that it's raining outside. I know very well that it's raining outside. Faith has nothing to do with it. Just like I know very well that the area of a circle is pi times the squared radius or that a punch in the nose can cause pain. Faith occurs only when the thing we have faith in defies our sense of what's possible or at least likely. So if someone has faith in Nessie or in Santa, I understand what that means, even if I think it's pretty peculiar and, indeed, profoundly unwise.

But again, whatever it is that you have faith in or that you have faith about, there has to be some idea of what that thing is.

So you cannot have faith in the existence of ghroblingats since you have no conception—absolutely no idea—of what it is that you might be having faith in. There is no idea of a ghroblingat; there's nothing to believe in. Faith in ghroblingats is impossible. So too for (Euclidian) triangles having more or less than 180 degrees. So too for justice having weight in ounces and pounds. And so too for God.

Again, you can utter the words. You can say "I have faith in the existence of God." You can say "I have faith in the existence of an exception to the rule that everything that exists must have been caused to exist by something other than itself." Those sounds can come out of your mouth. And by the same token, you can say "I have faith in the existence of ghroblingats" or "I have faith that I can draw a triangle having angles of either more or less than 180 degrees" or "I have faith that justice weighs three pounds and seven ounces." Those sounds too can come out of your mouth. But they're little more than noise, since there's no concept of a ghroblingat or of a triangle having either more or less than 180 degrees or of justice having weight in pounds and ounces. In each case, there's no idea in which to have faith, no intelligible concept. And so these are thoughts that you cannot have. They appear to be thoughts. We're talking about sentences that have the grammatical form that we use for expressing thoughts: subject, predicate, object. Indeed, that's almost certainly part of the problem. The grammatical form fools us into thinking that we're really saying something, that we're really expressing an idea. But we're not. Grammar is enormously important—it is, in fact, absolutely necessary for expressing an idea—but it's not everything. In order to express an idea, you need two things. You need a language—which means you need (among other things) grammar. But you also need an idea. Since there's no idea of something that both cannot possibly exist and absolutely must exist at the same time, all the language in the world cannot help you express that (non-) idea. And since faith requires some idea about which to have faith, faith in God is impossible.

You cannot have faith in the existence of a married bachelor. Think about it. What could it possibly *mean*? "Married bachelor." It's impossible that the term could ever apply to anything. So it's really just nonsense. "George has a wife and does not have a wife." Again, gibberish. Unlike Nessie or Santa, there's nothing *in which* to have faith because you're really not saying anything at all. You're not expressing an intelligible idea.

And so too for God.

At which point the atheist will say: "Right! Yes! That's the point! Exactly! You can't have faith in the existence of a married bachelor. And so, with respect to married bachelors, you must be a *non*-believer. You must *deny* the existence of married bachelors. Everyone who is married cannot be a bachelor; and there are no bachelors who have wives. And just as you must be a non-believer with respect to married bachelors, so too must you be a non-believer with respect to God. You must be an atheist. Right?"

But no. Not right. Not quite. Again, the problem with a married bachelor is not that it's impossible for a married bachelor to exist. The problem is that "married bachelor" is gobbledygook. If we're walking down the street and you say, "Oh look, over there, there's that married bachelor" or "I wonder how the bachelor's wife is doing" or "that woman is married to a bachelor," I'd think you were either crazy, making some kind of lame joke, or struggling hard—and, to this extent, unsuccessfully—to learn English as a second language. For whatever reason, you'd be talking nonsense. So when you say you don't believe that a married bachelor can exist, I honestly don't know what you're talking about. With respect to married bachelors, there's nothing the existence of which we would disbelieve. You might as well say you disbelieve in the existence of ghroblingats or in the existence of bxgzgktl. In each case, I wouldn't know what you mean. I could only respond with something like: "Huh?"

And so too for God.

According to certain standard views, Adam was punished because he had little faith. And more, he was punished because he was arrogant. He was arrogant because he disobeyed God and attempted to acquire a kind of knowledge that he couldn't have, namely, knowledge of good and evil and, by extension, knowledge of God. Eve convinced him to eat the apple. He shouldn't have done it, but he did. He did it because he didn't have enough faith in God and because he was arrogant. He thought that he could learn the truth about—have real knowledge of, a rational understanding of—God and the ways of God. So God got angry, punished Adam—and the rest of us have had to pay for it ever since.

What's interesting is that the story—like so many pieces of great literary art—contains a good deal of truth. By truth, I certainly don't mean that things actually happened as the Hebrew bible says. What I mean, rather, is that the author of the story puts his or her finger on a very fundamental truth about what happens when people talk about God. To claim to know—or to attempt to know—about the existence of God, one way or the other, certainly is the height of arrogance.

It is, however, an arrogance born of a certain special kind of ignorance.

Now let's be careful here. The problem is not that we're ignorant of God. The problem is not that we don't know enough about God. The problem is not that our knowledge of God is limited. The problem is not even that we can never know about God. Those are the agnostic's problems, and they're all false problems. Remember: it's false to think that our knowledge of God is limited. The problem is indeed a matter of ignorance, but I'm talking about a very different kind of ignorance. The real problem is that we are—at least all-too-often—ignorant of the fact that, when it comes to God, there is simply nothing to know. There is no concept of God. And certainly anyone who purports to have knowledge of, or seeks to have knowledge of, or even believes in a non-idea, a non-thought, something that is the functional equivalent of a ghroblingat—any such person must simply be ignorant of the fact that there is no concept.

But that's not quite it either. Because actually, deep down—in our heart of hearts, in our innermost mind—we know quite well that there's no concept of God. We're not really ignorant of that fact. Just as my buddy knows deep down that the Mariners won't win the pennant, so we all know in our bones that there's no idea of something that must exist and cannot possibly exist at the same time. The logic of cause and effect under which we all operate doesn't permit such a thought. So really what it comes down to is a kind of arrogance rooted in a failure to accept—a failure to recognize, to come to grips with, to acknowledge and face up to—the limitations of human thought. Certain things simply cannot be thought. Included among them is the idea of something that cannot possibly exist and absolutely must exist at the same time. No idea there. So when we continue to operate as though there were such an idea, we're living in a state of denial. We're being untrue to ourselves. We're lying to ourselves. We're being willfully ignorant, in the sense that we are willfully ignoring that which, deep down, we already know.

That's the problem with Adam.

Now I'd say the author of Genesis was a little too tough on Adam (though also on Eve). Maybe Adam was just a tad arrogant—an arrogance born of a certain special kind of ignorance. But we have to remember that he was, so to speak, under a lot of pressure—as are we. Adam, like us, wants the world to make sense, wants to understand, wants to *know*, what's going on. It's a perfectly natural impulse. Life is challenging, and it'd be nice to know that it all has some larger purpose. But we can't. Not without living a big fat lie. Knowledge of this kind is impossible.

And, of course, in the face of such an impossibility—in the face of what one might call the futility of Adam—we often turn, desperately, to faith.

Which brings us back to St. Paul. You'll recall from chapter 1 that Paul is important in thinking about the idea of faith. Faith was his big thing. Indeed, faith, for Paul, is largely what Christianity is all about.[1] But in light of what I've been saying here, you might wonder why he took this approach. Why faith?

Now according to Luke, it all happened in a flash. Literally. Of course, Luke—that's the Luke of the "Gospel According to St. Luke"—not only wrote his gospel but also (probably? maybe?) wrote the "Acts of the Apostles," which talks a lot about Paul. And as Luke tells the story, it all happened on the road to Damascus. Paul—he was called Saul at that time—was heading up there one day to persecute some Christians, since he was a very big anti-Christian. So there he is, traipsing along the road, when suddenly he's struck blind by an enormous bright light—the light of God. A direct, if not exactly explicit, message from God. And so, presto: he's converted. He has faith. Faith in God. Faith in Jesus. And the rest is history. That's Luke's account.[2]

But I myself have a sneaking suspicion that something else was going on as well. My guess is that Paul had this absolutely brilliant insight—maybe conscious, maybe not—that faith, blind faith, is really the only way to go if you ever want to have any hope at all of justifying a belief in the existence of God. And that's primarily because faith is—or, rather, seems to be—less dependent on the logic of cause and effect than any other theory. In particular, it seems to be less dependent on the logic of cause and effect than the two major alternative ways of thinking about God's existence that were floating around then: obedience to the law and knowledge of God's will.

The obedience-to-the law approach says we should believe in God because that's what the law requires of us—for example, the law of Moses that we find in the Hebrew bible. This, by the way, seems to be a teaching that you can find in the Gospel of St. Matthew, perhaps more so than in the other gospels of the Christian bible. But it won't do. It won't do because the law is, in fact, all about cause and effect. The law says: your action *caused* the sheep to be stolen—meaning, you stole it, pal—so we, in turn, we will *cause* you to go to jail. Rather than escaping the logic of cause and effect, the law sinks you deeper into it. And the alternative approach, the one that relies on knowledge—a profound, spiritual, perhaps mystical knowledge of God's will—is no better. It's no better because, in the end, knowledge of whatever kind generally involves knowledge about what causes what. Lisa has a terrific knowledge of automobile engines, which means she knows what *causes* engines to hum smoothly and what *causes* them to break down.

Either way—law or knowledge—you're pretty much stuck in the logic of cause and effect.

Faith—that is, faith in the existence of an Unmoved Mover—seems to avoid this problem. That's because it's so irrational. Now remember once again, the more bizarre the faith, the better. Faith is best when it doesn't make any sense. Faith defies, so to speak, rhyme or reason. But of course, the logic of cause and effect is just the opposite. It's all about making sense. It is, after all, a logic. So faith is, in a manner of speaking, free. You can believe whatever you want, unfettered by the need to think about causal relations. That, at any rate, seems to be Paul's hope. Indeed, that's his great project—or so I think. To escape the pitiless, inexorable logic of cause and effect.

But we're now in a position to see why this, too, won't fly. It won't fly because:

The second—the very instant—that you're talking about faith, you're talking about faith in something. In some *thing*. Can't be any other way. There's no such thing as faith in nothing.

And the second—the very instant—that you're talking about some thing, you're talking about *existence*. Because to be a thing is to exist. That's part of what it means to be a thing. Can't be any other way.

And the second—the very instant—that you're talking about existence, you're talking about *causation*. Because everything that exists was necessarily caused to exist by something other than itself. That's part of what it means for a thing to exist. Can't be any other way.

And the second—the very instant—that you're talking about all that . . . well you've obviously found yourself trapped once again in the logic of cause and effect. Which, of course, means pretty soon you're talking about something that absolutely must exist and, at the same time, cannot possibly exist. And by now we know where that gets us.

So now you see why I'm aproleptic—"without a concept."

By the way, one of the nice things about being aproleptic is all the neat stuff you can do with it. For example, when you're at a cocktail party and you tell people you're aproleptic and that you believe in aprolepticism, you can also tell them that you are, therefore, an aprolepticist and that sometimes you might even aprolepticize. All of which sounds kind of cool—especially when you go on to explain to everyone that, no, this doesn't mean you have some kind of delicate medical condition.

But being aproleptic has another nice advantage. It's correct. Indeed, it's the only view that makes any sense at all. And it's not only correct. It's correct in a way that puts you in touch with your own innermost convictions—with stuff that you already know deep down inside, but that you've kept hidden for one reason or another. Which, believe it or not, can be an enormously satisfying thing. Making sense—and that includes being at least roughly coherent—may not be a cure for all of our problems, but it sure helps.

8

IT'S ALL IN A GOOD CAUSE

Most of what I've said so far presupposes that all of us, pretty much all the time, think about things—and must think about things—in terms of cause and effect. Everything that exists must have been caused to exist by something other than itself. Everything, in other words, is an effect of a cause. Moreover, in all cases without exception, the cause comes first, the effect comes later. Maybe only slightly later—maybe only a split-second, maybe a nano-second—but later nonetheless. The effect cannot come before the cause.

But is all this really true? Are we really stuck with the logic of cause and effect? Can't we get ourselves out of that mindset? If we can change the world so that today someone in Athens can watch, in real time, a play taking place in Egypt, why can't we just change the way we ordinarily think about causes and effects? If we can imagine a world in which Santa can do his thing, why can't we just imagine a world where not everything is the effect of a cause, or where not every effect is preceded in time by its cause?

Because we can't. You can say we can. You can utter the words. You can insist. But as I've shown several times already, saying is one thing, actually doing another. In this case, the doing is impossible. Or so I think.

Imagine you wake up one morning, open your front door and find—unexpectedly—a package sitting there on the stoop. Just sitting there. You look around. Nobody. No truck. No person. Nothing there but the package.

Now this will likely give rise to any number of thoughts on your part. Do you remember hearing anything in the night? Did you order anything? It's not your birthday, is it? It's not Christmas, so it can't be from Santa, if there were a Santa.

And then, of course, you'll wonder: what's in the package? Is it something good? (Or, in this day and age, something really, really bad?) When did it arrive? Who brought it—UPS, FedEx, the mail? Did someone just drop it off? A friend? An enemy? Should I open it now or wait?

The next thing you'll probably do is inspect the outside. Is there a mailing label? The address of the sender? Is it something from Land's End or Amazon?

So there are a lot of things you might think. Maybe it's from Aunt Sue. Her famous cookies. Or maybe it's from my neighbor Joe, returning that bowl he borrowed (and deciding to wrap it up in a package since Joe, after all, is a neat-freak). Indeed, the number of things you might think is, depending on who you are and what the package looks like, pretty huge.

There's one thought, however, that you won't have and that you can't have. That's the thought that the package simply arrived from nowhere—sent by no one, brought by no one, accidentally dropped by no one or no thing. Just presto! A package—out of thin air.

When I say out of thin air, by the way, I don't mean figuratively out of thin air. Again, let's not get metaphorical. When we use the expression "out of thin air," we usually don't really mean out of thin air. We usually mean that we don't know—yet—where the thing came from. We're surprised it's there. In the case of the package, you didn't see a delivery truck or a person. So sure, you might say, "Geez, it just came out of thin air." But you know very well that it really didn't come out of thin air. It came from somewhere. There is no thing that comes from nowhere.

Something caused the package to be sitting there on your front stoop. The package sitting there is an effect of a cause. You don't—yet—know the cause. But the fact that there was a cause—some kind of cause—this you cannot deny.

Here's a test. What would happen if you denied it? I mean out loud, to your friends, or your neighbors, or your loved ones. I don't mean jokingly. I don't mean figuratively. I don't mean in the metaphorical sense of "out of thin air." I mean that you honestly and seriously and in all earnestness claim that nothing—absolutely nothing—caused the package to be sitting there. Not UPS, not the mail, not Land's End, not Amazon. Those would have been causes. No one just dropped it off. That would have been a cause. It didn't accidentally fall off an airplane and land on the stoop. That would have been a cause. It didn't happen to bounce off a delivery truck and roll up to the door. That would have been a cause. A sorcerer or magician or voodoo priest didn't make it appear. Those would have been causes—far-fetched ones, sure, but causes nonetheless.

So what if you seriously claimed out loud—you insisted—that none of this happened, nor anything else. Nothing caused the package to be sitting there. Absolutely nothing. You're not saying this is a mystery you haven't yet solved. You're not saying you don't know—yet—what caused the package to be there. You're not saying the appearance of the package was due to supernatural causes—note, supernatural *causes*. You're denying all of that. You're saying—again with deadly seriousness—that nothing caused the package to be there. It simply appeared.

I'm pretty confident that if you said that, your friends or neighbors or loved ones would—as, shall we say, a straightforward matter of cause and effect—immediately begin to worry about your mental health. And with good reason. For the thought that nothing caused the package to appear on your doorstep is a thought that you cannot have—if you're sane and not a very young child.

What's true of your package is equally true of everything else you encounter, everything else that happens to you. Indeed, it's true of everything that exists—anywhere, anytime. No thing can come from literally nothing and nowhere. Everything is the effect of a cause.

Let's think a bit more about "out of thin air." Again, it's a phrase that we use figuratively, not literally. When we say that the package just appeared out of thin air, we mean we don't know where it came from—but we know that it came from somewhere and that something caused it to appear.

But there's another problem with thin air. The problem is that thin air—literal, not figurative, thin air—is not nothing. It's something—and this can help us see, I think, just how absurd it would be to insist that something can come out of nothing.

For if we're going to take this notion of nothingness seriously, then we have to agree that when we say nothing, we mean really, really nothing. No air. No chemicals. No molecules. No atoms. No subatomic particles. No elementary particles. Complete and total emptiness. The utter absence of anything. Absolutely, entirely, and completely nothing. Because if it's not the utter absence of anything, then it's not nothing.

For example, if there is a single atom—and if that's all there is—then that's not much. But it's not nothing. Far from it. It's something. Really something. It's a thing that exists. It is, in some sense, a hunk of matter. A really small hunk, but a hunk nonetheless. And of course, if an atom exists, even if it's the only thing that exists, then this simply raises the question: where did it come from? What caused it to come into existence? In fact, the atom is pretty much like your package. It couldn't have come into existence out of absolute, total, complete nothingness. Something must have caused it to exist. But then—here we go again—what was that pre-atom thing and what caused *it* to come into existence? And so on, ad infinitum.

Thin air—if it's really thin air—is hardly nothing. However thin it might be, it's chock full of stuff. Not just atoms but, at one extreme, subatomic particles of which atoms are composed and, at the other extreme, molecules that are composed of different atoms. Lots of molecules in thin air. Those molecules exist. They are substances, things, hunks of matter even larger than atoms. As such, they must have come from somewhere. Something must have caused them to exist.

If your package somehow really did come out of literal thin air, then you'd have to ask (at least) the following: where did thin air come from?

Evidently some—or many—physicists believe that before the world existed there was nothing. I myself know virtually nothing about physics, so that perhaps explains my confusion. But my confusion is this: how could nothing have existed? What does that even mean? Evidently some—many—physicists really mean that before there were atoms, there were other things. Photons, quarks, neutrons, electrons, nuclei. Elementary particles. The appearance of an actual atom, it seems, came a long way down the road. That's okay by me. If they say so, I'll buy it. But then one still has to ask: where did those elementary particles come from? If something called the Higgs particle really is the building block of all matter, as some physicists seem to believe, who am I to argue? I defer. Sounds good. Count me in. But then I have to ask once again: where did the Higgs particle come from? What caused it to come into existence? Do physicists really believe that it came literally out of nothing—absolutely nothing, zilch, zero, the complete and total absence of anything, of any particle, subatomic or otherwise? For if they believe that, then they've lost me—exactly as you've lost me if you insist that the package on your doorstep came from nothing and nowhere. The Higgs particle, or whatever is the building block of matter, cannot have simply appeared out of thin air—either literally (because thin air already has lots of atoms) or figuratively (because no thing can come out of nothing).

Some—most?—physicists believe that the shape of the world today is the result of a Big Bang, occurring maybe fourteen billion years ago. Other physicists apparently disagree. Nobody knows for sure. I certainly have no opinion. If in fact the world as we know it was the result of a Big Bang, I say great. Works for me. But if there was a Big Bang, surely something had to bang. My mind simply cannot wrap itself around the notion that there was, at one point, absolutely nothing, no molecules, no atoms, no elementary particles, absolutely and positively nothing; and so I can't wrap my mind around the idea that it was nothing that banged. If there was a Big Bang, then some thing—however amorphous, however formless, however undefined—must have existed; and whatever it was that existed must have existed before the Big Bang itself. But of course, if something existed before the Big Bang, then something else must have caused that something to exist. And so on, ad infinitum.

Lots of very smart people today—including lots of very smart scientists—say that we don't need God to explain the world. Science does the job. Big Bang, evolution, DNA—all of that stuff is all we need to account for everything. God is totally superfluous. Just do science.

A lot of atheists make this argument. Now I've already shown why I think atheism doesn't work. To assert that God doesn't exist, which is what the atheist (often) says, is to claim that something—some intelligible thing—doesn't exist. To deny the existence of something is to say that there is an idea, a comprehensible idea, but no factual counterpart to that idea. Like Nessie or Santa. In each case we have the idea, but we don't believe that the idea describes anything that actually exists in the world. That's what it means to disbelieve in the existence of something. Like Nessie or Santa. Sometimes, as with Nessie, we just don't think the thing actually exists; at other times, as with Santa, we don't think it could possibly exist. But in either case, we know what we're talking about. We have an idea. God, however, isn't like that. The idea of God is not an intelligible idea at all. It's gibberish. So just as there's nothing to believe, there's also nothing to disbelieve. You might as well say that you don't believe in the existence of ghroblingats, or in the existence of bxgzgktl—in which case, I'll say that I don't know what the heck you're talking about. You're just making noise, like a barking dog.

But some atheists are also fond of saying that they're atheists because science provides a much better explanation—a cleaner, simpler, more straightforward account of the universe. To which I say, again, I don't know what you're talking about. Now I actually think these people aren't really saying what they think they're saying. What they're really saying is that science can provide a perfectly adequate account not of the universe but of the shape of the universe. The world looks today the way it looks—it has the stuff it has, the form it has, the structure it has—because of Big Bangs and evolution and DNA and so on. And that seems to me just fine. I'm happy to agree that we are the way we are today, and the world is the way it is today, and things have *developed* the way they've developed today, all for reasons that science has explained—or that science will explain as it gets better and better at explaining things.

What this means, by the way, is that I absolutely agree that science does a much better job of explaining the shape of things than the so-called theory of intelligent design. The theory of intelligent design says—roughly—that the world is so marvelously and intricately constructed, so beautifully and artfully put together, that it couldn't have happened by accident. It must have been the result of a very powerful designer. But if science can explain that marvelous and intricate structure, if it can account for the seeming beauty and art of the world, then surely we should go with science—something we understand and see and that makes sense—rather than intelligent design. And I myself have very little doubt that science can do precisely this. Science—which is, after all, the most rigorous example of the logic of cause and effect—is just better at explaining how we got where we are than anything else.

But accounting for the *shape* of the universe is not the same as accounting for the *origin* of the universe. It's not the same as accounting for the very *existence* of the universe. It's not the same as explaining how things got started in the first place—by which I mean in the *very* first place. And here, it seems to me, science is as hopeless as anything else. Again: something must have banged. Or: evolving organisms must have evolved out of something. Or: the DNA molecule didn't just appear out of thin air—by which I mean not thin air but literally nothing and nowhere. You see: every scientific account of the shape of the world, however powerful and persuasive, nonetheless presupposes the existence of the world. It *presupposes* the existence of something that *then* got shaped—banged, evolved, etc. And that's okay. But of course, by presupposing the existence of the world, science begs—as it must beg—the fundamental question that we're asking: where did the world come from in the first place? As far as that question is concerned, science leaves us exactly where we were without science. The world must have started, so there must have been a First Thing, but there can't have been a First Thing since that First Thing must have been caused by something other than itself, and so on ad infinitum.[1]

Recently, a few scientifically oriented folks have tried ever more creatively—or ever more desperately—to get around some of these issues. Implicitly recognizing problems posed by the logic of cause and effect, they've posited the idea of a universe that existed before the development of space and time. In the beginning, they tell us, it's not simply that there was nothing. Rather, it's that there was really, really, really nothing. These folks are proposing, in effect, a radically new view of nothingness. For them, nothing means nothing at all. No photons or quarks. No neutrons, no electrons. No Higgs particles. Not even an empty vacuum. Just—well—nothing. And that means not only no objects. It also means no space. Literally. Space did not exist. No left and right, no up and down, no east and west, not even a here and a there. And there wasn't any time either. No hours, no minutes, not even a nano-second. No present, no past, no then, no now. Back in the good old days, so to speak, time didn't fly, and it didn't stand still either. It simply didn't exist at all. This was, supposedly, the time before time.

The basic idea seems to be that if there was, in the beginning, no space and time, then we really don't have to bother about cause and effect. After all, causes precede effects in time; the cause always comes first, the effect later. And the cause is always distinct—physically distinct, in space—from the effect. If they weren't distinct, then it wouldn't make any sense to call one thing a cause and the other an effect; in a world of cause and effect, it takes two to tango. Of course, as we've seen, all of this is a problem if you want to explain how the world got here. But if, before the world existed, there was no space and no time, then presto, problem solved. Cause and effect? Nothing to worry about. Unmoved Mover? Don't need it. God-talk? Irrelevant and superfluous. Science does the job all by itself.[2]

Sometimes this is called "post-relativist cosmology." I myself might call it something else, but I'll restrain myself. I'll restrain myself in part because I'm too polite. And I'll restrain myself in part because I honestly don't know what these people are talking about.

If they're talking about what things were like in the beginning—or what things were like before the world existed—then it sure looks like they're presupposing time. After all, "beginning" is a time word. So is "before." Hard to get away from it. Hard to talk about the time before time without talking about, er, time. And if these folks are talking about what things were like in any sense whatsoever, then it sure looks like they're presupposing space. You tell me: what kind of "things" are they that don't exist in space?

And if they want to insist on a circumstance—a condition? a situation? a state of being? a world? a universe—that preceded (oops, another time word) or that existed outside (oops, a space word) of space and time, a world where there is truly nothing, then I wonder what it could mean to call it—notice, "it"—anything at all.

And if somehow there could truly be a world of nothing—no objects, no space, no time—then the same old question would remain: how could objects have emerged in the first place? From where did the elements of which objects are composed come from? Remember, even if the very first objects arose randomly, without any systematic rhyme or reason, totally as a matter of luck, it still seems to be the case that they necessarily came (past tense) from somewhere (spatial concept). Can't imagine how it could have been otherwise.

Of course, you can say that before the world existed there was absolutely nothing. You can utter that sentence, just like you can utter a sentence saying that justice weighs three pounds and seven ounces on the scale or that the number three smells bad. Those words—those sounds—can come out of your mouth. But as we've seen, the fact that you can utter a sentence doesn't mean you're saying anything other than gibberish. And it doesn't show that all of this post-relativist cosmology is not an elaborate, self-referential, hermetically sealed—though perhaps amusing and entertaining—system of high-level wordplay that gives the appearance of saying something important when, in fact, it's not saying a darn thing.

In the end, then, it's hard to see now this new cosmology is any different from the old cosmology. If you can show me how we can have a concept of a world that is devoid of everything including space and time, how we can have a thought according to which objects arise out of absolutely nothing at all, how we can have the idea of a world in which there is no here and there, no then and now—if you can show me how any of this can translate into something intelligible, please let me know. I mean it. I'm serious. Drop me a line. Send me an e-mail. You can even text me. God knows,

I'd love to be proven wrong about all this. I'd love to be shown that there really are big ideas out there and I'm just not smart enough to see them.

Of course, if I'm not smart enough to see them, then it's hard to imagine how I could be smart enough to understand if and when I've been proven wrong. And that could be a problem. A serious problem. I don't deny it. But what can I do? Remember, the whole point of this book is to figure out here what kind of thoughts are possible for an ordinary person to have. And if, as an ordinary person and certainly no scientist, I'm just too dopey to comprehend how, for example, something can come out of nothing, then so be it. I'm trying my best folks, but I am who I am. And given who I am, I can't for the life of me see how what we're dealing with here is anything other than dueling mumbo-jumbos—the mumbo-jumbo of God-talk versus the mumbo-jumbo of scientists who, frustrated by the first kind of mumbo-jumbo, have stopped doing science.[3]

It's perhaps ironic, but the logic of cause and effect underwrites most—maybe all—religious thought. Of course, given the ubiquity of that logic—given the fact that all ordinary humans think about the world in terms of cause and effect—it could hardly be any other way. But it seems ironic nonetheless.

So again, the very notion of God as the Unmoved Mover is driven by the need to explain how the world could have been *caused* to exist. No such notion would have arisen if we didn't understand, deep down, that making sense of the world means attempting to explain the world as the effect of some cause. The fact that the logic of cause and effect also and at the same time undermines the notion of an Unmoved Mover doesn't change the fact that it, the logic, is responsible for it, the notion (which, again, turns out not be a notion at all).

Consider, in this context, the religious beliefs of the ancient Greeks, as embodied in the works of Homer. It's actually a very useful case, because Greek religion could hardly be more different from the monotheistic—as one says, Abrahamic—traditions that most of us are used to. Greek religion is polytheistic. The gods have distinctive personalities. They have specific jobs. This one handles the grain, that one handles oceans, a third takes care of the wine, and so on. They have emotions—feelings of love, jealousy, sexual desire, and so on—that seem a lot more human than divine. Pretty different from the God of Judaism (whether of Abraham or of Job, themselves two very different things), or of Christianity, or of Islam.

Now I should say it's true that Aristotle, who spoke of an Unmoved Mover, was also an ancient Greek. But Homer was an even more ancient Greek—preceding Aristotle by, perhaps, four hundred years. And it's pretty clear that the views and images that we find in Homer's poems were the views and images that dominated everyday life in Greece, both in the archaic period (roughly 750 BCE to 480 BCE) and in the classical period (480 BCE to about 350 BCE).[4]

If you read the *Iliad* and the *Odyssey*, you find not only mortals interacting with mortals and gods interacting with gods but also mortals and gods interacting with one another. The great hero Achilles was, of course, the offspring of a mortal father and a divine mother. So yes, Homer's gods copulate with mortals as well as with each other. But they also talk with mortals, giving them advice or warnings or predictions or other information that might help or hurt them. All of this helps explain why people in Homer do the things they do. A lot of the time, it's because the gods tell them what to do.

More important, however, is the fact that a lot of things happen in the Trojan War—according to Homer—because the gods make them happen. Or, to put it perhaps more appropriately, the gods themselves directly cause lots of things to occur. For example, in the middle of battle one spear happens to hit its target while another happens to miss. Of course, sometimes this is simply caused by the skill, or lack of skill, of the warrior who threw the spear. Achilles himself could handle a spear pretty well. Others weren't so good. In spear throwing as in basketball dunking, some have it, some don't. But sometimes all the skill in the world doesn't seem to help. In Homer, skilled warriors sometimes miss. And at other times, folks without much skill at all do pretty well. So what's up with that? Luck? Pure chance? Not for the Greeks.[5] According to Homer, what seems like luck or chance turns out to be a god deciding that the spear should or should not be on the mark. The gods interfere with things. One god takes an errant spear and decides to redirect it in midair, resulting in a dead warrior. Another god diverts an on-target spear from its intended victim, thereby saving a life. He or she causes this or that to happen.

Everything that happens in the *Iliad* is an effect that has been caused by something other than itself. Homer and presumably his listeners (Homer was probably an oral, improvisatory poet whose works were actually written down only much later) certainly operate under the logic of cause and effect, same as us. And the cause is very often human. But if it makes no sense for a human to have caused a thing to happen, then for Homer, and for the Greeks, there's only one alternative: a god must have caused it. And bear in mind, this is true not just of spears and warriors in the *Iliad.* In the *Odyssey*, it's winds and seas and sailors. God only knows how many times Odysseus himself is thrown off course by raging oceans and howling gales, shipwrecked on desert islands, and thereby prevented from getting home to Ithaca. Navigational mistakes? Meteorological flukes? Inexplicable tsunamis? Forget about it. It's really the gods—for example, the god Poseidon, angry at Odysseus—who makes all that bad stuff happen.

So notice once again: the logic of cause and effect doesn't necessarily mean scientific cause and effect. Modern science is, indeed, a manifestation of that logic. But so is belief in magic and sorcery, in astrology and alchemy, in voodoo and witches, in the occult and paranormal—and in God, or the gods. Obviously these various things differ wildly from one another. Principally they differ in terms of how they conceive of evidence and how they understand what is, and is not, Physically Impossible. But in all cases, the endeavor is driven by the need to figure out what causes what in the world. And that need reflects nothing other than the universality of the logic of cause and effect.

But is it really as universal as I'm suggesting? Aren't there cultures that operate entirely or substantially outside the logic of cause and effect? Am I not overgeneralizing? Am I not being ethnocentric—a typical Western, not-quite-dead white male?

A friend—not my Seattle Mariners friend but a different friend, one who has absolutely no interest in and no knowledge of the Mariners or anything else having to do with baseball or any other sport—recently visited a very large city in what we call "the developing world." She described a city that seemed to make no rhyme or reason, a city of chaos, a city without rules—or at least effective rules—that appeared somehow to function in ways utterly foreign to the Western mind. She adamantly denies that these people operate in terms of cause and effect. The logic of cause and effect is, well, logical. It is orderly. It is systematic. Even if it produces nutty ideas like gods bending spears or sorcerers casting spells, it still says: here's a cause, there's an effect; the one produced the other and did so in a particular way and in a particular time sequence. My friend claims to have experienced in this large city of the developing world no such orderly thought, no such effort to create a coherent system, not even a clear sense of time. It's all a jumble, an ongoing, disconnected series of happenings, a world filled with disorder—and with disorderly thinking. For her, the logic of cause and effect is far from universal.

Now, just as I'm no theologian—and no physicist, and no mathematician—I'm also no anthropologist. So maybe my friend is right. But I have my doubts. I know, for example, that the very large city she described is filled with buildings. Oodles of buildings, some small, some enormous, some old, some new, some well-built, some poorly built, but all of them standing up, at least for the time being. People live and work in those buildings. The buildings function at least roughly as buildings do in our neck of the woods. They keep out the rain. They keep people warm. They provide security. And if they do none of these things perfectly, that's certainly true of our buildings as well. So I ask myself—and I ask my friend—how did those buildings get there unless someone decided to build them? And once someone decided to build them, how did they get built? I don't see how a building gets built unless somebody says something like: "If we do this—say drive a nail or lay a foundation or saw a board or lay a brick—then that will happen; and if we do something else, a different thing will happen; and if we do lots of these things, and do them in a particular way and in a particular sequence, the result will be walls and floors and ceilings and—ultimately—a building; so if we want a building, then I'll do

X and you'll do Y and she'll do Z, and so on." Which is another way of saying: "All these activities—X and Y and Z—will cause the building, which doesn't exist, to exist. The building will be an effect of those causes." We call that the logic of cause and effect, and I don't see how the building gets built any other way.

Now the people of this large city in the developing world may well have very different views of what's actually causing what. They may think that the activities of workers are being caused by the gods or by sorcerers or by magic. Their understanding of how things work—and, thus, of what's physically possible and what's not—might be profoundly different from ours. But however that may be, it seems that they still must be operating under the logic of cause and effect; and I'll bet that, just like us and just like the ancient Greeks, they make some effort to systematize causes and effects in order to make sense of what's really going on in the world, at least as best they can. And of course, this isn't just a matter of building buildings. These are people who cook their meals and fight their wars and play their games and—to get really, really basic—go from point A to point B. Hard to see how they do any of that without having some sense—however inchoate, ill-defined, or peculiar—of a causal schema, such that if I do this, then that will happen. And whatever the context, whatever the theory, whatever the underlying explanation, the idea that "if I do this, then that will happen" is a case—indeed, a paradigmatic case—of the logic of cause and effect.

So does all this mean that I'm a strict determinist? Does it mean that we're all strict determinists? If we all operate under the logic of cause and effect, does this imply that we don't believe in freedom? Am I making an argument against free will?

In fact, I am not. But this is a complicated issue. While it takes us rather far afield, it can't be completely ignored. I'll try to be brief.

First, I'm not sure we have free will and I'm not sure we don't. I don't know, and I doubt that anyone does. How can one say for absolutely sure that your seemingly free decision to do something was in fact not free at all but was caused by some deep forces—your culture, your subconscious, your libido, an evil demon—about which you're entirely unaware? I don't think one can be certain either way, and it may be that we will never be certain either way, though I'm not sure about that. So you see, with respect to free will (as opposed to God) I am—believe it or not—an agnostic.

But I'm more than that. For I also believe that any normal life, and any normal society, involves a whole range of things—notions of good and bad, of right and wrong, attitudes of resentment and anger and disgust and gratitude and admiration—that frankly presuppose free will. In other words, we act *as though* there were free will, even if we're not sure there is free will. For example, if you do something that seems gratuitous to me and that harms me, I'm liable to feel resentful of you. Feeling resentful in such a circumstance is the most normal thing in the world. It's a perfectly natural response. Of course, if I became convinced that in fact you really had no control at all over what you did—if your action was entirely caused by something and someone else, say an evil demon, hence was in no way a product of your free will—then I shouldn't feel resentful toward you at all. And indeed, I wouldn't. Resentment, at least resentment toward you, wouldn't make any sense. It wasn't your fault—you had no control—so I can't blame you for what happened. But, in fact, I sometimes *do* feel resentful toward you and toward others; and this means that while I don't know if we have free will, I regularly and routinely act as if we do. And it seems to me, moreover, that that's true not just of me but also of you, and of society as a whole, and of every society of which I'm familiar. So if I'm agnostic about free will, I also believe that the very idea of society—with its rules and prohibitions, its punishments and rewards, its praise and blame—presupposes what cannot be proved, namely, that we have the capacity to make choices, free choices, for which we are, in the end, responsible.[6]

But notice something else. If I freely do something that causes something else to happen, that's a matter of cause and effect. In other words, there's no obvious contradiction between the logic of cause and effect and the (I think unprovable but not obviously false) presupposition that we have the capacity for free will. Free will can itself be a cause; indeed, that's pretty much what it is. Think about it. What else could free will be but the *cause* of the things that are done under its direction?

Now you'll object. Okay, if free will is the cause of the things that are done under its direction, then what's the cause of free will itself? Indeed, the very idea of free will is that its decisions are *not* caused by anything other than itself. It is *self*-determining. It is, we sometimes say, autonomous. As such, it's not the effect of something else. Free will, if it exists, thus breaks the chain of cause and effect. It undermines the logic of cause and effect.

All of that's fine. But notice something else. Even if we have free will, even if free will is real, it has to reside *in* something or, more likely, someone. Free will is—at least according to our lights—a faculty that something or someone *has*. You're free or I'm free or we're free; but in any case, *someone* is free—if, that is, freedom exists. The concept of free will just existing out there, independently of any person or of anything like a person, just doesn't make sense. That's not and that cannot be free will. And that's important.

Because if free will must reside in something or someone, then of course that something or someone must itself exist. And if that something or someone exists, then—oh yes, here we go yet again—something must have caused that something or someone to exist, and we're back in the logic of cause and effect.

But what if you want to insist—bizarrely—that free will could exist in the world on its own, apart from anyone or anything? I have no idea what that could possibly mean. If you want to insist on it, however, you're still saying that something—the faculty of free will—exists, in which case I'll pose the same questions: where did it come from, what explains its existence, what caused it to exist? The idea that everything that exists is an effect of some cause other than itself applies to *everything* that exists. Simply saying that something exists out there that was completely uncaused—whether it's an Unmoved Mover or some kind of independent faculty of free will—is not to make it so. You can utter the words—you can make the sounds with your mouth, you even formulate grammatically correct sentences—but that doesn't mean you're making sense.

So if I'm right about all this, why can't we simply change our way of thinking? If human thought—whether or not it accepts free will—operates under the logic of cause and effect, what would happen if we just decided to think differently? Why can't we just unthink our current way of thinking? If we can imagine the real existence of Santa, if we learn to make flying machines, if we can invent television so that we can watch plays being performed thousands of miles away in real time, why can't we think of new ways to think?

But look carefully at what I've just said. Why can't we *think* of new ways to think? The problem is that the only way to think about new ways to think would be to, well, think. But to think means to employ our way of thinking. If our way of thinking is governed by the logic of cause and effect, then we could undermine the logic of cause and effect only by relying on the logic of cause and effect—our way of thinking—and that means not undermining but, rather, reaffirming the logic of cause and effect.

Consider a more general problem. That's the problem of the relationship between human thought in general and the real world out there. Over here we have humans—you and me—thinking about all that stuff over there in the world; and over there we have, yes, the world itself, with all its stuff. Trees and buildings and animals and other people and so on. The tough question is: how do we know we're thinking about that stuff correctly? How do we know we've got it right? How do we know that what we say about trees and buildings and animals and other people is actually true? What, in short, is the relationship between human thought on the one hand and things in the world on the other? How do we know that human thought isn't really and totally off-base?

Tough question. It's maybe the toughest question of all, something we have to think about. Trouble is, we can't think about the relationship between human thought on the one hand and things in the world on the other except by using—what else—human thought itself. We're humans. We think. And when we think, we use—and cannot help but use—human thought. That's what it means for us to think. There's no other option for us. That's all we have. So it's impossible—literally impossible—for us to have an *independent* perspective on the relationship between human thought on the one hand and things in the world on the other. Any perspective we have—and any thinking we do—will always, eternally be from *within* the perspective of human thought. There's no breaking out. We're trapped. We're stuck. If we try to think of a way out, that means that we humans will be thinking, and when humans think they think from the perspective of human thought.

As Jean-Paul Sartre, the French existentialist, once said in a not so different context, there is "no exit."

To the degree, then, that I'm right—to the degree that ordinary human thought operates under the logic of cause and effect—there's simply no way to unthink that since, again, any thinking we do will use, hence will be hostage to and dependent on, the logic of cause and effect.[7]

That's where we are. That's what we're stuck with. That's the—capital letters here—Human Condition. We might not like it, but sorry to say, there really isn't anything we can do about it.

But don't despair! If it sounds bad, it's not. In fact, as I already suggested several times, all of this—everything I've been saying—is really, really good news. You'll see. I promise.

9

DETECTIVE FICTION

Before we get to the good news, however, there's one item that needs to be cleared up.

Some people will insist that the account I have presented thus far is perfectly consistent with a certain way of believing in God. Specifically, what I'm ignoring is the idea of "mystery." Yes, some critics will say, God is a mystery indeed. A deep, dark mystery. But because something's a mystery doesn't mean it's impossible; and it certainly doesn't mean you can't believe in it.

This, apparently, is what they used to teach kids in certain parochial schools. Maybe they still do. I'm not sure. My wife, at any rate, says that's what the nuns taught her and her classmates at good old Holy Names. God, they said, is a mystery. How can there be an eternal being? It's a mystery. How can there be an omnipotent being? A mystery. How does God do what He does? A mystery. (And yes, at Holy Names it was always a He.) So, they said, let's not try to figure it out. Let's just believe. We don't have to get caught up in logic or in questions of cause and effect. Can't explain God and the universe? Don't worry. It's just a mystery. Is the real truth beyond our mortal comprehension? Of course it is. Who could deny that? But this doesn't mean God doesn't exist or God is impossible. Indeed, all it shows is how really great God is.

That's what they said at my wife's parochial school. Maybe they still do. And it sounds reasonable at first. But really, it won't do. You see, the idea that God is a mystery is, well, not an idea at all.

So what, in fact, is a mystery? Well basically, a mystery is something to be solved.[1] Of course, this doesn't mean that all mysteries actually *are* solved. They're not. But nonetheless, that's the basic idea of a mystery—to solve it.

Think, for example, about the mysteries of Sherlock Holmes or Miss Marple or Sam Spade. Murder mysteries. I myself happen to be a kind of murder mystery nut. Always was. I loved Sherlock as a kid.[2] In college, Hammett was my man. *Maltese Falcon*? The absolute pinnacle, in my opinion. Later, when I lived for a few years in Southern California, I went through a Ross Macdonald phase. And then there was—is—Maigret, he of the Quai des Orfèvres.

Every murder mystery is a whodunit. That's the word we use. A "whodunit." And, of course, that's the question. Who dun it? That's what a murder mystery is all about. That's what the detective is trying to discover.

But look closely at that word. Whodunit? It presupposes an "it"—*something* happened. And it presupposes a "who"—*somebody* did it. The whole idea of a murder mystery is to find out who. Of course, we also want to figure out how. And maybe why. But the how and the why are mainly useful for finding out the who. It's the who that really counts. Now what's important to notice here is that there's absolutely nothing about a mystery that involves Conceptual Impossibility. As a matter of fact, there's nothing that involves Physical Impossibility either, or any other kind of impossibility. Indeed, the whole idea of a murder mystery is that there's no impossibility at all. To the contrary: we know perfectly well that there's a straightforward, unproblematic, easily comprehensible answer to the question. The truth is not only possible. It's necessary. Someone did it. It's as simple as that. We just have to find out who.

A murder mystery—like any other mystery—presupposes the logic of cause and effect. The logic of cause and effect poses no problem for the detective. It doesn't present any hurdles to be overcome. In fact, it's exactly and precisely the opposite. The idea of a whodunit is nothing other than the idea of a cause (the who) and the effect (the dead body). So the logic of cause and effect is actually wonderful for the detective—it's the detective's best friend—because it means that every effect absolutely must be the result of some preceding cause. Just as someone or something must be responsible for the package on your doorstep, so must someone or something be responsible for that corpse over there. Can't be otherwise. The gumshoe knows without any doubt whatsoever that the mystery is solvable—provided only we get enough facts. There absolutely must be an answer. *Someone* killed the poor schlub.

What makes a murder mystery mysterious is not Conceptual or Physical Impossibility. What makes it mysterious is that, for the moment, we don't have enough information. And we don't have enough information, in part, because the murderer is trying to hide things from us. The perp—the typical perp, anyway—wants to get away with it. So he or she figures out how to destroy evidence or establish an alibi or frame an innocent person or do anything else that will fool us. And what this means is that when we try to solve the mystery, we're simply employing good old-fashioned cause-and-effect reasoning in order to distinguish the phony causes—the killer's deceptions—from the real ones. That's what Sherlock Holmes did. He used logic to analyze the evidence. Elementary, my dear Watson. The victim's dead body—the effect—is over there. Lying on the rug or the sidewalk or wherever. Let's just find the cause.

The problem with God is virtually the opposite. The problem with God is not that we don't have enough facts. The problem is that we don't have an idea at all, and so we can't even know what kind of facts we should be looking for. Facts about what? To look for facts about God would be like trying to put justice on a scale and weigh it in ounces and pounds. What exactly would we place on that scale? It would be like trying to draw a (Euclidean) triangle having more or less than 180 degrees. How would we even begin? What kind of investigation would we undertake? Where would we start?

Now one problem with what the nuns told my wife in parochial school is that they didn't really stick to their guns. They were not consistent. They said God is a mystery, something beyond human comprehension, too complex, too difficult for our poor noggins—but then, in the very next breath, they said some other things, in fact lots of other things. They said that God is up there, in heaven. They said that God is good—really, really good. They said that God is merciful. And that God loves us. And has a Son. And is omniscient. And is omnipotent. And will forgive our sins. And will punish evil. And is vengeful. And is a He. And is everywhere. And—well, we can go on and on. So while they told my wife and her classmates that God is a mystery, they also gave Him an address, a psyche, a philosophy, an attitude, a gender, a family, and tons of other stuff besides. Not much of a mystery after all. God is here, or there. God is like this, or like that. God does this, or does the other thing. Mystery largely solved.

But, of course, mystery not solved.

Okay, then, suppose we just get rid of all that other stuff. God is neither good nor bad, neither up there nor everywhere, neither loving nor vengeful, and so on. Let's not say anything at all about God. Except that God exists. That's the one thing we'll say. And it's a mystery that God exists. Can't explain it. No evidence for or against. Hard to believe. But nonetheless, God exists. And that, simply, is the mystery. After all, we're here. The world is here. Something must have caused it. It's a mystery, but that's just the way things are. We live in a mysterious universe.

Again, that's definitely not what they told my wife at good old Holy Names. But maybe that's what they should have said. Of course, without all that other stuff—God's geography and His psychology and His kinfolk and His mind-set and so on—it would have been pretty difficult to construct a doctrine, hence pretty hard to create a religion. But that doesn't make it wrong, does it?

No, that doesn't make it wrong. But it's wrong nonetheless. It's wrong because it's saying that the Unmoved Mover is a mystery. It's saying that it's a mystery that there can be something that exists that caused the world but that itself was not caused to exist. That's the supposed mystery. But in fact, it's not a mystery. It's nonsense. Gibberish. There's no idea there, and so there's nothing to figure out. There's no mystery to be solved, since the thing—the idea of an Unmoved Mover—is not a coherent, intelligible idea at all.

Let me run all this by you again, very briefly, just to make sure there's nothing mysterious about any of it. For every mystery—whether it involves Sherlock or Hercule or Lieutenant Columbo or whomever—we always know, we absolutely know, that there's a solution, a correct answer. While we might not be able to discover it—again, some murderers get off scot-free—we nonetheless know that it's out there, somewhere. But more: we know exactly what *kind* of answer it is. It's a cause-and-effect answer. The butler did it. Or the jealous niece. Or the tall, dark stranger. *Somebody* did it. We just have to find out who.

But as we've seen, with the Unmoved Mover—with God—it's exactly the opposite. We have no idea what *kind* of answer we're looking for, and that's because we really don't know what we're talking about. And we don't know what we're talking about because, in fact, we're not talking about anything. We're just flapping our gums. Gibberish. Mumbo-jumbo.

Really, though, the point is actually much stronger than this. Because, you see, we *do* know—we absolutely know without any doubt—that we can't be trying to discover what caused the world to come into existence. That *can't* be our goal. It can't be our goal because we know that something must have caused the world to come into existence—the world exists and everything that exists must have been caused to exist by something other than itself—and so there absolutely must have been a First Thing, an Unmoved Mover, which of course means that the First Thing or Unmoved Mover must have existed and therefore must have been caused to exist by something other than itself, which in turn must have been caused to exist by something other than itself, and so and so on, which means that it's simply impossible that there could have been a First Thing or Unmoved Mover, and so the First Thing or Unmoved Mover absolutely must have existed and at the same time absolutely cannot have existed—all of which describes not a mystery to be investigated or a problem to be solved but a conceptual mess, an incoherence, gibberish. Mumbo-jumbo.

Now it's true that we cannot explain the world. To that extent, what they told my wife in parochial school was, I suppose, perfectly fine. We can't make sense of the world. Impossible. But that doesn't mean the world is a mystery. To the contrary, it means something very different. It means that the problem of explaining the world is much greater, much more severe, much more extreme, much more radical than any mystery could ever be. Remember: the idea of a mystery is the idea of something that makes sense but that we just can't quite figure out. Yet. But the problem of the world is a problem that really doesn't make sense. And so there's nothing to figure out. It doesn't make sense because the moment we try to state what the problem is, we're actually failing to state what it is. The problem is how something absolutely must exist and cannot possibly exist at the same time, and that's not an intelligible problem. The moment we try to put it into words, we get caught in a tangle of contradictions. The moment we say that it's a mystery or a puzzle or a question, we're saying that it's something to be investigated (like any mystery) or solved (like any puzzle) or addressed (like any question)—and the moment we say any of that, we're immediately saying that we're trying to find the cause of the world. Which—since the world must have been caused and cannot have been caused—is impossible. Conceptually Impossible. Gibberish. There's no idea there.

There's really nothing, literally nothing, that we can say about the problem of God without turning it into something it's not—a mystery, for example.

In the face of all this—in the face of our inability even to identify a real problem to be investigated—what do we do? How do we react? How do we respond? What do we say? What should we think?

Well, it seems to me there's only one thing to do. And that's to forget about it. I mean that literally. You should just banish the whole thing from your mind. Ignore. Swallow your tongue. Pay no attention. Change the topic. Think about something else. Punt. Don't waste your time. Move on to more important things.

Which, it turns out, is not simply good advice. Believe it or not, it's also really the best news one could imagine.

IO

AN INKLING OF . . .

In a very strange and very surprising way, Plato—yes Plato, of all people—points us in the direction of good news. This is strange and surprising because Plato wrote before the problem with God was a recognizable problem, at least recognizable from our point of view. It's strange and surprising because Plato was, of course, one of the very earliest contributors to the Western tradition of serious thought—meaning he was one of the ones who got the whole thing going—and you'd have imagined that by now his writings would have become long since obsolete.[1] They're not. And it's strange and surprising because, in the end, Plato really doesn't give us a very good answer. He makes many of the same mistakes that so many others have made. But despite all this, he has a particular and peculiar insight about God-talk that turns out to be extremely helpful. I myself think the guy had an epiphany.

Something hit him like a ton of bricks. Right there in Athens. A ton of bricks.

I'm afraid you can't understand Plato's view about God, however, without spending at least a little bit of time with Socrates, his teacher and mentor. In particular, you can't understand Plato without thinking about the hot water that Socrates got himself into precisely on the question of God, or the gods. But it's even worse than that. Because I'm afraid you can't understand the problem of Socrates without knowing at least a little bit—not much, but a little bit—about Socrates's world.

Now we've already looked at Homer and his view of the gods, back in chapter 8. But in fact, it's a poet named Hesiod, roughly a contemporary of Homer—we're talking in the vicinity of 700 BCE—who really gives us the clearest picture of ancient Greek religion. And a pretty weird picture it is.

Hesiod is actually famous for two important poems. One is called "Works and Days," which is, you might say, the very first attempt to produce a farmer's almanac. It's a compendium of homely, everyday advice for the average Joe—or the average Spiros—who's trying to scrape a living out of Greek soil, no easy job. Hesiod talks about agriculture, household management, how to behave in society and a slew of other things. As such, the poem is especially important for historians. For example, Hesiod explains to his readers how to behave at a dinner party. Seems a simple enough topic. But in fact, this tells modern-day historians something they might otherwise not have known, namely, that the Greeks of the seventh century BCE actually had dinner parties, pretty much just like us. If the Greeks didn't have dinner parties, Hesiod wouldn't—couldn't—have written about them; and if he hadn't written about dinner parties, we might not have known that the Greeks had them. "Works and Days" is, in short, a tremendous source of information about everyday life back then.

The other poem is called "Theogony," and it's the story of the gods. Here's where Hesiod tells us who the various individual divinities are, where they came from, what their world is all about. And the first thing to say about "Theogony" is that Hesiod completely punts on the question of the origins of the universe. It's not that he doesn't offer a creation story, because in fact he does. But the story he offers is, I'm afraid, all too familiar, nothing you haven't already heard a hundred times over. And if Hesiod is one of the first writers, if not the very first, to present this particular story, that doesn't make it any better. To be specific, he tells us that everything started in Chaos. That was the beginning, the First Thing. Complete and utter Chaos. That's what Hesiod says. And then out of this Chaos came Earth, and then everything else. Of course, the trouble is that Hesiod never tells us where Chaos came from. Presumably Chaos is an incoherent mess. It's a bunch of stuff that's, well, chaotic. But of course, if there's stuff, even chaotic stuff, then the stuff existed; and if it existed, then something must have caused it to exist. And Hesiod never tells us what. Worse, he never even acknowledges the problem.

From this beginning in Chaos, by the way, Hesiod comes up with all kinds of mumbo-jumbo. His account of things is, from our perspective, about as wacky as it gets. Consider, for example, the birth of Aphrodite, the goddess of beauty and sexual desire. According to Hesiod, the original leader of the gods was Ouranos. Ouranos was, at the beginning or near the beginning, the boss, the big enchilada. And so there he was, sitting up at the very pinnacle of the godly pecking order, ruling the universe with an iron hand, the original alpha male. Now the interesting thing is that Ouranos was not only tremendously powerful; he was also a bit paranoid. On the one hand, the guy was a control freak, and a bully. But at the same time, he was always looking over his shoulder, and he was especially afraid of his own children. That, of course, seems pretty strange. After all, what kind of alpha male is it who's scared of the kids? But then again, maybe, just maybe, it wasn't so strange. Maybe Ouranos had good reason to be looking over his shoulder. Because it turns out that, in fact, his own son, Cronos, actually was out to get him. Yes, Cronos had it in for daddy, perhaps because he—Cronos—wanted to be the alpha male; and in the end, the son got the father, but good. To make a long story short, Cronos castrated the old man and threw the testicles into the sea, whereupon sperm from the testicles mixed with the water to create foam, and out of the foam emerged—somehow—the goddess Aphrodite.

That, my friends, is the kind of thing poor Socrates—a perfectly sensible and highly rational person who lived about three hundred years after Hesiod but whose society still believed in the kinds of stories Hesiod told—was up against.

Of course, a lot of us can relate. A lot of us are reasonably sensible and rational persons who operate in terms of cause and effect, and yet we live in the world where people, probably most people, claim to believe there's a God—that is, a First Thing, an Unmoved Mover, who might or might not look like a cross between Karl Marx and the Dude—even though, deep down, they really don't believe that at all, since it's impossible that there was and also impossible that there wasn't a First Thing, which means there's no such idea. And at the same time, we live in a world where a great many other people claim to believe that in the very beginning, before the Big Bang, there was something like Chaos—all kinds of chemicals and other stuff, just floating around—which they don't really believe either, since if there was Chaos, then Chaos existed, and if it existed, then something before Chaos must have caused it to exist, and so on ad infinitum.

So Socrates is going down the street one day on his way to court. By this time, he's an old man. And he's gotten himself into a bit of a pickle. Somebody has accused him of a serious crime and he's going to have to defend himself in court. But before he gets there, he runs into an acquaintance named Euthyphro, and they strike up a conversation. Socrates can't resist a good conversation.

Now Euthyphro is an earnest and serious young man who has a moral dilemma. The problem is that he thinks his own father, a well-heeled landowner, may have been responsible for the death of an employee. The details are unimportant. What's important is that Euthyphro suspects his father is guilty of what today might be called negligent homicide. Euthyphro's not actually certain that his father is to blame for the poor man's death. But there's lots of circumstantial evidence, so this is probably something that needs to be tested in a court of law. On the other hand, Euthyphro also loves and respects his father. And of course, he owes his father, big time. After all, it was his father, along with his mother, who caused him to exist in the first place, just like my parents caused me to exist and my friend Vivian's parents caused her to exist. Of course, his father also raised him, sent him to school, bought his clothes when he was a kid, and did all kinds of other good things for him. So Euthyphro's dilemma: should he rat out his father or should he keep his mouth shut? If he rats him out, he's being disloyal to pops. But if he keeps his mouth shut, he might be letting a criminal get away with murder, or at least with negligent homicide.[2]

Euthyphro and Socrates, it turns out, agree that this might be a question of piety. And they agree as well that whatever Euthyphro does, he should do the pious thing. But Socrates wonders: what is the pious thing? Certainly piety means being religious, and being religious means doing what your religion requires you to do. But exactly what is that? Of course, for both Euthyphro and Socrates it probably means, among many other things, respecting your father. Having respect for your parents—honoring thy father and mother—seems like the kind of thing most religions want you to do.[3] For Euthyphro and Socrates, anyway, that's a no-brainer. But the trouble is that piety probably also means respecting the law and respecting justice. Making sure the guilty get punished seems like a really pious thing to do. Religions generally preach justice. But this means that Euthyphro and Socrates are stuck: which one—protecting the old man or ratting him out—does piety really require? You can't do both.

Now our dynamic duo agree that they can't answer this question unless they know exactly and precisely what piety is. So that's the basic problem: what is piety? Really and truly. And it's a problem that turns out to have enormous significance for the problem of God.

Think about some analogous circumstances. The First Amendment to the Constitution of the United States says that the government shall make no law infringing freedom of speech. So does this mean you can yell "Fire!" in a crowded theater if you want to? Does it mean you can commit libel and slander with impunity? Does it mean you're allowed to publish, produce, and display obscene and pornographic materials any time and any place you want—say, right in the middle of downtown at Christmas time, next to the big department store with its Santa and its dominoes and its five-year-old children? In one sense, all of these things seem like "speech," and yet none of them is allowed, at least not in the United States. So of course we have raging controversies all the time about what the First Amendment means. And that's interesting because the First Amendment—the part about speech, certainly—is really about as simple as it gets. "Congress shall make no law . . . abridging the freedom of speech." That's it. One can hardly imagine a more straightforward assertion. Nothing complicated there. But the key question is not so simple: what constitutes speech? What kinds of things qualify as speech, and what kinds of things—even if they look and sound like speech—don't?

It's pretty much the same with piety. We know—Euthyphro and Socrates know—that to be pious generally means to be religious, to do what religion expects and demands of us. But just as it's not always clear to us what speech is, so it's not immediately clear to the Greeks—or to us—just what it is that religion requires.

Obviously this is a question about the gods, and about the world that Hesiod described—the world in which Euthyphro and Socrates find themselves. So how do they, Euthyphro and Socrates, proceed? Well, the simple answer is that they proceed pretty much exactly the way we've been proceeding here, in this book. They do philosophy. And they do philosophy pretty much the way we've been doing philosophy. Specifically, Socrates is trying to determine what he and Euthyphro really believe about the gods, deep down. In particular, he tries to separate what Euthyphro thinks he believes—what he, Euthyphro, consciously thinks and actually says—from his, Euthyphro's, real, underlying convictions.

Socrates's mechanism for doing this is pretty clever. He begins by asking Euthyphro what he thinks piety is, and Euthyphro gives Socrates an answer. Euthyphro tells Socrates what he consciously thinks about piety. He says that piety is nothing other than what the gods love. He—Euthyphro—expresses a thought, the thought he has at the moment. Whatever the gods love, that's piety. It's really not a bad thought. After all, surely the gods like to be worshipped; so to be pious, to be worshipful of the gods, would seem to be pleasing to the gods. They love it. That's Euthyphro's thought. And just like my friend's thought that the Mariners will win the American League pennant, it's a real thought. An honest-to-goodness, comprehensible, initially plausible thought.

But just like my friend's thought, it's also not what Euthyphro himself really thinks, deep down. And just how do we know that? Well, after Euthyphro says that piety is what the gods love, Socrates then asks him another question. He asks him if the gods always agree about everything, and Euthyphro has to admit that, deep down, he believes the gods disagree with each other. A lot. In fact, Euthyphro—presumably a faithful student of Hesiod—really believes that the gods fight with each other on a fairly regular basis. Sometimes a god who is a son even castrates another god who is his father. So the gods are not of a single mind. Some of the gods love certain things, and others of the gods love other, different things. What pleases one god might make another god really, really angry. And if that's so, then it becomes difficult to believe that piety is simply what the gods love. Euthyphro—because of Socrates's question—now realizes this. He realizes that the thought he expressed is not consistent with, doesn't accurately reflect, what he really believes, deep down. So he has to get rid of that thought and try to come up with another one that's more consistent with—that's faithful to—his own innermost commitments.

The conversation that Euthyphro and Socrates have about piety is very short—only about fifteen pages in my English-language edition—but pretty much the entire conversation is composed of Euthyphro providing different definitions of piety, one after the other, and Socrates asking questions designed to see, in each case, if that's what Euthyphro really believes, deep down. In all, we encounter six definitions of piety (depending on how you count), and each one turns out to be a dud. Upon reflection, in other words, each one is inconsistent with Euthyphro's own innermost convictions, and so each one has to be discarded. We call this the "Socratic method."

Now there's an additional feature of this little conversation that's really important. As I say, the whole exchange is only about fifteen pages long. But it ends very abruptly. Euthyphro—his sixth and last definition of piety having just been shot down because it's inconsistent with his own deep beliefs—seems frustrated by the whole thing. He's had enough. Enough talk. And enough feeling stupid in the face of Socrates's questions. He just wants to get on with things. So he abruptly terminates the conversation and leaves.

What's important about this is that at the end of the whole conversation we still don't know what piety is. And neither do Euthyphro or Socrates. We've learned that some proposed definitions of piety are really bad definitions. But we still don't know the right definition. And that's a real problem. It's a real problem because, at the end of the conversation, we don't have the slightest idea whether or not Euthyphro should bring his father's actions to the attention of the court. And Euthyphro clearly doesn't know either. His conversation with Socrates hasn't answered his question. In fact, it may have left him more confused than he was before.

The discussion that I've just described was written up by Plato in a very short work—a dialogue—called "Euthyphro." And remember, it's Plato's epiphany that we're looking for. It's Plato's epiphany that's going to give us a clue to the good news that I've promised you. So Plato's really the person we're interested in. But I hate to say it: before we get to Plato, we still need to know a little more about Socrates. Because what happens to Socrates in court is crucial to explaining and understanding Plato's epiphany.

Everyone knows that Socrates was condemned by the city of Athens to drink the hemlock and die. Which he did. But there are several other things to remember about this.

First, the trial of Socrates was deeply enmeshed in Athenian politics. And Athenian politics in those days were pretty brutal. Cutthroat, hard-nosed, take-no-prisoners politics. Left-wingers versus right-wingers. At least part of the reason for this was that these were tough times in Athens. For one thing, the trial of Socrates occurred in 399 BCE. This was only five short years after the end of the Peloponnesian War between Athens and Sparta, a truly horrible, brutal, and devastating war that had lasted for twenty-seven years. It was also a war that the Athenians lost in devastating fashion. Athens surrendered in 404 BCE, badly beaten.

Now after the surrender, a pro-Spartan government was established in Athens. This government was called the Thirty Tyrants. Athens had been a democracy for decades,[4] but losing the war allowed the anti-democrats—the tyrants—to take over. The most important leader of the Thirty Tyrants was a fellow named Critias, and here's an absolutely crucial fact about Critias: he had been a devoted student of Socrates. A protégé. A star pupil, even. One might say—one might at least guess—that Socrates taught Critias everything he knew. So Critias the tyrant was a product of nothing other than a Socratic education. And in the eyes of many Athenians, that didn't make Socrates look any too good.

There's another important fact about the political situation that you need to know. Athens lost the war probably because of a controversial and ultimately calamitous decision to send a huge army halfway across the Mediterranean to Sicily. A big chunk of the Spartan army was in Sicily, so the thought was: let's fight them over there, far away from Sparta itself, rather than close to home, which will improve our chances. Seems sensible enough, but the result was actually an unmitigated disaster. The Athenian army in Sicily was virtually wiped out. Tens of thousands killed—and these were not pretty deaths. It really was a horrendous business. Although the war lingered on for another nine years, Athens was essentially finished after Sicily. Its fate was sealed. Now the most important and influential proponent of the so-called Sicilian expedition was a glamorous, beguiling, charismatic fellow named Alcibiades. Young, handsome, silver-tongued—it was Alcibiades indeed who convinced the Athenians to go to Sicily; and as you might imagine, when the disaster happened, his reputation took a big hit, to say the least. But to make matters worse, just as things were going south in Sicily, Alcibiades actually defected to the other side. He took off and joined up with the enemy. He joined the Spartans. A traitor. Now the punch line: Alcibiades had also been a student and protégé of—guess who—Socrates. Another troubling, and highly visible, product of a Socratic education.

So consider the bottom line. Socrates was the teacher of—the inspiration for—both Critias the tyrant and Alcibiades the traitor. Not a great record. All of which meant that when democracy was restored in Athens, which actually happened pretty quickly, lots and lots of people came to think of Socrates as a fellow-traveler of the anti-democrats, a preacher of tyranny, and even a secret Spartan sympathizer, hence a possible traitor, at least in his heart. Yes, this was guilt by association. But the association was pretty strong.

Now the main accusation against Socrates was that he was a heretic. A religious heretic. That was his supposed crime. Actually, there were several charges in the formal indictment. But the most important of these was that he was guilty of corrupting the youth of Athens—just as he had corrupted Critias and Alcibiades—by encouraging them not to believe in the gods. Originally, this meant that he was charged with heterodoxy—with believing in the wrong gods, not the official gods, hence with attempting to undermine the recognized and established religious beliefs and practices of Athens. And one would have to say, in retrospect, that this was actually a pretty credible charge. Because, as I've already indicated, Socrates was a sensible and rational fellow; and as I've also said, the recognized and established religious beliefs of Athens—goddesses being created out of sperm floating in the ocean, and such—were not so sensible and rational. Socrates, like me, hated mumbo-jumbo; and the world according to Hesiod, the official religious world of Athens, certainly was a mumbo-jumbo world. So heterodoxy was the original charge, for which there was, let's admit, a fair amount of circumstantial evidence.

But during the course of the trial itself, the man prosecuting Socrates—a fellow named Meletus—actually accuses Socrates not of heterodoxy but of atheism. Meletus in effect changes the indictment, which was a perfectly legal thing to do in ancient Athens. It's not clear, by the way, why Meletus changes the indictment. Maybe he really believed that Socrates was an atheist or maybe he just got mad at Socrates during his cross-examination, lost his temper, and made a tactical mistake. In any case, it certainly seems to have been a tactical mistake. That's because Socrates has no trouble refuting the accusation of complete atheism. Specifically, he can say with a straight face and perfect honesty that he's always talked very publicly and openly about gods, that he's always done so with great respect, and that he's often told people how gods have inspired him to do philosophy. Of course, he doesn't say which gods. He doesn't defend himself against the charge of heterodoxy. But since that charge is no longer in operation—again, the new charge, according to Meletus, is atheism—it doesn't matter. Or shouldn't matter.

On the other hand, maybe Meletus didn't make such a tactical mistake. After all, Socrates is, in the end, convicted. Not only is he found guilty, he's also condemned to die. Now there's a huge and very old dispute about just why he was convicted and condemned. Certainly part of the reason is that Socrates, in court, behaves badly, or at least unwisely. He shows no remorse. None at all. In fact, just the opposite. He's defiant. He tells the jury something like the following: "If you folks let me go on the condition that I stop practicing philosophy, I promise to ignore the condition. Because as long as I'm alive and free, I'm going to practice philosophy, no matter what you people say." Not exactly diplomatic.

Maybe Socrates thought he was calling the jury's bluff. But if so, the strategy didn't work. The jury, it turns out, wasn't bluffing.

Now it certainly seems likely, given all the facts, that the jury—which, remember, was a democratic jury—was simply convinced that Socrates was at heart an anti-democrat and a Spartan sympathizer. We've seen circumstantial evidence to that effect. They were prejudiced against him on political grounds. But it's also likely, and maybe even more important, that the jury was deeply suspicious of Socrates's views of the gods. Everyone knew that Socrates—a very public intellectual—was constantly investigating things, questioning things, being skeptical about things, trying to figure things out. Socrates accepted nothing on faith. And remember, faith is, or so I think, at the core of religion. Not just St. Paul's religion, but religion per se. So someone who accepts nothing on faith, someone who just rejects the idea of blind belief, is someone who is, in principle, a threat to religion—especially if that religion is as peculiar and unlikely as the religion that was described by Hesiod, foam and all.

Consider again, just for a moment, Socrates's conversation with Euthyphro, which—remember—took place right before the trial.[5]

Because if you think about it, it seems pretty obvious that Euthyphro's initial instinct is the correct one. His initial instinct is to bring his father's case to court. After all, if his father is guilty of a crime, it really shouldn't matter that he, Euthyphro, is his son. Guilty is guilty, crime is crime, and a basic sense of moral decency and moral duty suggests that it doesn't matter if you are friends with, or even closely related to, the guilty party. Justice needs to be done. Criminals can't be allowed to get away with their crimes. That's Euthyphro's initial intuition, and an excellent intuition it is. That's the belief in which he has faith. But after about a ten-minute conversation with Socrates, Euthyphro is no longer so sure. Socrates has confused him. One might suggest that he has forced Euthyphro to overthink the problem. He has made Euthyphro doubt his own best instincts, his own strong moral intuitions. Socrates has undermined Euthyphro's faith in common sense. And that seems to be a natural result of, hence is an inherent problem in, Socratic philosophizing. Socrates sows the seeds of doubt. That's what he does. He's a skeptic. He's looking for proof, even where absolute proof is unlikely or impossible. He undermines received beliefs. And it's for that reason that Socrates is a threat to Athens itself. Heterodox indeed. Given Socrates's way of thinking about things and talking about things—as, for example, in his conversation with Euthyphro—it certainly would have been easy for the jurors to think that, deep down, Socrates doesn't believe in any god at all, not the gods of Athens and not any other gods.

All of which is a problem for Plato.

Plato was born into a distinguished and venerable Athenian family. The elite. His stepfather was a gentleman named Pyrilampes, who was a crony of none other than Pericles, the greatest Athenian politician of his age, indeed perhaps the greatest of any age,[6] and one of the most important democratic figures of all time. Plato's own biological father—who died when Plato was still a boy—was also an important figure in politics. And you remember Critias the tyrant, mentioned a few moments ago? He was Plato's second cousin. Moreover, it doesn't stop there. Another one of the Thirty Tyrants, a fellow named Charmides, was Plato's uncle.

Now all of this means, among other things, that Plato—a young man of ability—would have been expected to pursue a life of politics. Plato himself makes no bones about this: "When I was a young man," he once wrote, "I expected, like many others, to enter directly, as soon as I was my own master, into the public life of the city." Plato's family certainly would have wanted him to follow in the footsteps of his father and stepfather and to assume, thereby, the prerogatives and responsibilities of his station.

But Plato didn't do that. Like Critias and like Alcibiades, he became a student, protégé, and devoted follower of Socrates. But unlike them, he became a philosopher himself. Of course, he was Socrates's greatest student by far. But he was also the most loyal—a real Socratic, through and through. He adopted not only Socrates's manner of thinking but also his way of life, a life that's decidedly nonpolitical, maybe even antipolitical.

Now all of this necessarily put Plato in a ticklish position. Or several ticklish positions. Here's a young man destined for big things in politics who gives up politics altogether for a life of philosophy. And Socratic philosophy at that. Instead of choosing a life where he'd be doing things—drafting policies, making decisions, ordering people around, wielding power—he chooses a life of thought. Instead of the rough and tumble of politics, he opts to spend his life with books and ideas and Socratic conversations. His family must have been deeply disturbed. Plato, after all, was in complete rebellion against everything his folks stood for.

Of all the problems Plato had, dealing with the question of the gods and religion surely would have been one of the toughest. If Socrates was a rational and sensible fellow, Plato was, if anything, even more so. Here was a man who hated mumbo-jumbo of all kinds, whose life was devoted to getting at the truth of things, who subjected all kinds of mythologies to withering criticism. But Plato surely realized at least two other things. First, he realized that taking on religion—expressing doubts about the gods, about things like foam and Aphrodite and all that—could get a person into deep trouble. In fact, it could get a person killed. Plato had witnessed what happened to Socrates up close. It had to have affected him. Discretion being the better part of valor, it's easy to imagine Plato deciding to be very, very careful about expressing any kind of religious skepticism at all. But second, he also was committed to a way of thinking about things—and a theory of the world—that simply had no room for Greek religion at all. Plato was not a big fan of Physical Impossibility. He was not a big fan of Conceptual Impossibility, or any other kind of impossibility. And he was, most emphatically, a cause-and-effect kind of guy. He was convinced that the world actually makes sense, and that human beings could figure out the sense that it makes. In particular, he was absolutely convinced that there was something—some underlying principle or process or entity—that held everything together, something that made all the pieces of the universe fit together in a coherent, intelligible way. Of course, the question was what.

And here, I think, is where Plato had his epiphany. It's an epiphany about God, and it's an epiphany that Plato comes to express by using a grand metaphor. That—the metaphor part—is important. Plato doesn't tell us exactly what the underlying principle or process or entity is because he doesn't really know what it is. But he thinks he knows the *kind* of thing it must be. And so, in order to express the kind of the thing it must be, in order to give us a feel for what it must be, even if we really can't say and really can't know what it must be, he gives us a metaphor.

The metaphor is the sun. The underlying principle or process or entity functions like the sun. Now what does that mean? Well, Plato wants to say a number of things about the sun. First, the sun is what makes it possible for us to know anything about the world at all. This is because the sun allows us to see. If there were no light—no light at all—then we couldn't see anything. I mean really, really no light. Total darkness—which is, Plato thinks, pretty much where we'd be without the sun. If we were in total, complete darkness, we couldn't see anything; and if we couldn't see anything, then we couldn't distinguish anything from anything else. We couldn't tell the difference between a bum and a streetlamp, or between a ground-rule double and a three-hopper to third, or between a package sitting on the stoop and the stoop itself. We couldn't see anything at all without at least some light; and without the sun, there'd be no light. Everything would be completely and totally black. And I think we'd have to agree that Plato has a point here. After all, without the sun there'd be no moonlight, since moonlight is nothing but a reflection of the sun. Without the sun there wouldn't be light bulbs, because we can't manufacture light bulbs unless we can see what we're doing and for that we need the sun. And without the sun, there'd be no fire—except, perhaps, on rare occasions involving lightning storms—

because without the sun we couldn't find two sticks to rub together. So the possibility of our seeing anything at all absolutely depends on the existence of the sun.[7]

But second, there's actually one thing, one very important thing, that we can't see—at least not with the naked eye—and that's the sun itself. We cannot look directly at the sun with the naked eye. If we tried, we'd go blind. It's really an amazing fact that all of us are aware of, that we live with every day, and that for Plato is really, really interesting and really, really crucial. The sun is always there. It makes vision—indeed, it makes life—possible. We know where the sun is. We know what it does. But even though it's always there, right there, hanging up there, over our shoulder, rising every morning in the east and setting every evening in the west, we cannot ever look at it, at least not with the naked eye. We can never have direct access to the sun.

And what this means, finally, is that, according to Plato, we really can't say much about the sun at all. Of course, for technological and scientific reasons, the situation has obviously changed dramatically. We now have all kinds of ways of inspecting the sun and figuring out what it's made of. But just think about things from Plato's point of view, and from the point of view of the ancient Greeks in general. From their point of view, while you know the sun is up there and while you know pretty well what the sun can do—you know how crucial the sun is—there's not a whole lot more you can know. And not a whole more you can say. The inability to look directly at the sun—to experience the sun the way we experience streetlamps and ground-rule doubles and packages and stoops—means, at least for Plato and his contemporaries, that anything you say about the sun is necessarily going to be kind of vague, limited, incomplete, imprecise and, indeed, metaphorical. Yes, it's up there, way up there. I can feel it. I can glance in that direction. It gives off light. An enormous, unbelievable amount of light. It's huge and incredibly powerful. It lets us see. We couldn't live without it. But beyond that, what is it? How did it get there? What's it made of? Exactly how does it work? Why does it exist? And Plato's response to all of that is: who knows? If we can't see it—and if we can't approach it, eyes open, and put our hands on it and feel it and experience what it's like, up close—we can't say much about it. We know it's there, we know what it does, and that's the end of it. Case closed.

For Plato, God is—metaphorically—just like the sun. Pretty much everything Plato says about the sun, and pretty much everything he *refuses* to say about the sun, applies pretty much identically to God. Huge? Yes. Incredibly powerful? You bet. Even more powerful than the sun? Way more powerful. God makes everything possible. God makes the world intelligible—visible not to the eye but to the mind. God doesn't cast physical light like the sun but casts a different kind of light: a moral light, a rational light, an orderly light. The world makes sense because of the intelligent luminosity of God. Indeed, we couldn't live without God. The distinctions that we make—between correct and incorrect, between logical and illogical, between right and wrong, between good and bad—couldn't be made without that intelligent luminosity. But at the same time, though for different reasons, we cannot look directly at God. Never can and never will. Plato says that God's intelligent luminosity is so great that if we tried directly to look at it, we'd be intellectually blinded, just like we'd be physically blinded if we tried to look directly at the sun. Now I don't know exactly what it means to be intellectually blinded, but clearly Plato wants to say that we really can't possibly—can't ever—know very much about God. We can't know how God got there, what God's made of, how God does what God does, why God exists. In fact, Plato even hesitates to use the word *God*. Because that word—the word *God*—tends to conjure up misleading images of divine, immortal persons and sons castrating fathers and foam in the ocean growing into beautiful and powerful spirits and all the rest of that mumbo-jumbo. None of that will do. So what Plato really has in mind is an underlying principle or process or entity. Like the sun, we know it's there—it must be there, otherwise the world wouldn't make any sense—but, beyond that, there's virtually nothing to say.

This, then, is Plato's ingenious solution. Presumably it's a solution that could help save him from suffering the same fate that Socrates suffered. Because no one can accuse him of atheism. Just as he affirms, as he must affirm, the existence of the sun, so he affirms, as he must affirm, the existence of God. He's a believer. Devout and pious. But at the very same time, his particular account also lets him escape the mumbo-jumbo. It lets him retain his intellectual self-respect. Because he's making no ridiculous claims about foam or anything else. Indeed, he's offering almost nothing in the way of description. He sticks to his guns much more firmly than the nuns at good old Holy Names did. He is, to a very considerable degree, mumbo-less and jumbo-less. Thinking back now to Euthyphro and Socrates, Plato has found, or thinks he's found, a way to be really and truly pious and, at the very same time, to be logical, rational, and coherent. He's found a way to have his cake and eat it too.

Unfortunately, in saying what he says, Plato actually says too much. Much too much. Because even to talk about an underlying principle or process or entity, rather than to talk about God, is nevertheless to talk about something that exists. And if it exists, something else must have caused it to exist; in which case the underlying principle or process or entity isn't really underlying at all but is, rather, dependent on an even more underlying principle or process or entity, which in turn is dependent on some still more underlying principle or process or entity; and so on ad infinitum. Plato cannot escape the logic of cause and effect and the problems it causes for God-talk, all God-talk, even hedged God-talk.

But Plato nonetheless senses the problem. And that's where the sun metaphor comes into play—the metaphor of something that we know is there but that we cannot possibly see, ever. It's a deeply imperfect metaphor. It really doesn't work. But it sheds light on things. It's a metaphor that, for all its limitations, leads the way.

Which is, yes, really, really good news.

II

. . . THE TRUTH

We want God to exist because we want to make sense of the world. And we want to make sense of the world because we want to know who we are and how we got here and what we're supposed to do and why we're supposed to do it. We seek guidance and we seek meaning.

We want to live in a world where life—our life—has some larger purpose. Because the thought that there's really no larger purpose is, at least for many of us, pretty troubling. The thought that the world is nothing more than a system of purely physical causes and effects, a vast and random collection of atoms and molecules and various other hunks of matter, some of it inanimate, some biological, some large and some small, rocks and trees and insects and frogs and bipeds (human and otherwise) and Nessie (if he ever decides to show up) and Santa (if we can only figure out the technology) and all the rest, constantly bumping into each other, lacking rhyme or reason, flying around hither and yon, back and forth, to and fro, seemingly without direction, until each hunk of matter, one by one, its energy dissipated, slows down and stops bumping, stops reacting, stops moving altogether and then, at long last, exhausted and weak, disappears into nothingness, into the deep, dark hole of an impassive universe, ashes to ashes, dust to dust—that's daunting stuff. Whether we admit it or not—and if we don't admit it it's usually because the alternative is too disturbing—we want, desperately want, the story to have a moral, a larger meaning. And we want to know what role we play in that story. How do we fit in? What's our purpose? What does the script have in mind for us? Because if we knew that, if we could figure that out, then at least we'd have a chance to figure out some other things as well—like what to do, how to act, what kind of life to live, what kind of person to be, what's important, what's trivial, what to care about, what to ignore. And maybe we'd have a chance to figure out why any of it matters in the first place.

And so here comes God. The great thing about God is that now we can have a story, a story with a moral. We can have a story with a moral because now we have an author. God's the author. And what an author! He's got a role for everyone. Literally everyone. He assigns to each of us a function, a goal. And he's also omnipotent, all-powerful. He's an author who can actually put everything—all of His ideas and characterizations and plot-lines and narrative devices—into action. He (She? It?) can make it all real.

So you see, God obviously put us here, each of us, for a reason. God tells us what to do, how to live. God gives significance and purpose to life. God provides direction. We're not alone. The universe is not empty. It's not silent. God loves us, will take care of us. Indeed, on some accounts, God will provide for us eternally.

Alas, there is, sorry to say, no idea of God. God is Conceptually Impossible. Of course, since there's no concept of God, there's nothing about which we could say either that it exists or doesn't exist. We can neither believe nor disbelieve in God's existence. But this also seems to suggest that—as far as we can tell, from the perspective of human thought—we're pretty much back to being alone. All alone. Floating around aimlessly until we're floating no more—living, and then dying, in this immense, cold, dark, hollow, soulless universe, tiny specks in an infinitely huge expanse, an expanse that goes on and on, forever and ever, eternally, stretching out to nowhere.

As the old song had it: "What's it all about, Alfie?" And it looks like the answer is: it's about nothing at all.[1]

If that doesn't give you the willies—maybe not now while you're reading this, but perhaps at night, while you're lying in bed, and it's dark, and you're contemplating your own mortality and the vast emptiness of the galaxies, and you know that before too long you'll no longer exist, not really, and you'll be moldering in your grave, your consciousness snuffed out forever, no more thoughts, no more ideas, not even any ideas that are not really ideas, no more you, not ever, gone, forget it, goodbye—if that doesn't give you the willies then nothing will.[2]

Philosophers sometimes call this angst. Or anguish. Or dread. Another, simpler word would be fear. Pure, naked, unalloyed, unavoidable, paralyzing fear. Fear of the empty, bottomless, unavoidable, eternal abyss.

But take heart.

Because the fact of the matter is: there must—absolutely must—be something more than this. I don't state that as a matter of opinion. It's not a guess, nor is it a hope. It's not an article of faith. Let me repeat that: *it's not an article of faith.* I certainly don't intend it to be a question of religious belief. It is, rather, a simple matter of fact. Objective fact. Undeniable. True.

Actually, there are two facts.

The first fact is that the logic of cause and effect is completely and entirely and utterly and eternally unable to explain the universe. The universe exists. Something must have caused it to exist. There must, absolutely must, have been a beginning. But there cannot have been a beginning since, under the logic of cause and effect, if there was a beginning, then the beginning existed, which means that it must itself have been caused by something else, which in turn must have been caused by something else, and so on, ad infinitum. All of which is an impossible, irresolvable paradox.

The second fact is that the universe exists. It may not be what we think it is. I might be a brain in a vat, and everything else might be a figment of my imagination. But even then, something exists, and therefore the universe exists. This we cannot possibly deny.

And that's a really, really important fact. Because if the universe exists—as it clearly does—then something has to explain it. There must, absolutely must, be an explanation. Somewhere.

Of course, the explanation of the universe cannot be a matter of cause and effect. The logic of cause and effect fails miserably to explain the universe. It simply does not—and never can—do the job. Not even close. So there's really one and only one possibility: there must be Something Else. Not a First Thing. Not an Unmoved Mover. Not God. That's impossible—Conceptually Impossible. But Something Else. By which I mean something outside of, external to, different from, inexplicable in terms of the logic of cause and effect.

It's a pretty simple idea, but it's also really important, so let me run it by you again. The world exists. There just has to be an explanation. The logic of cause and effect can't provide the explanation. So there must be Something Else.

Now the second I say that—the second I say "there must be Something Else"—I have to take it back. Immediately. Instantly. Right away. I can't say it and get away with it. Because it's incoherent nonsense. Gibberish. Mumbo-jumbo. I've been accusing everyone else of mumbo-jumbo, and here I am doing it myself.

So I take it back. Pretend I never said it. My mistake.

And why is that? Why is it mumbo-jumbo? Well notice. When I say "there must be Something Else," I'm saying, explicitly and unambiguously, that there's something—some *thing*. Even if I'm not saying what that thing is, I'm nonetheless saying that it's *some* thing. Of course, I'm also saying, as I must be saying, that it *exists*. That's what the word "be"—as in "there must *be* Something Else"—indicates. And as we've already seen, the second—the very instant—that I start talking about something existing, I'm right back in the logic of cause and effect. Again, that's because everything that exists must have been caused to exist by something other than itself, and so on ad infinitum.

So when I say "there must be Something Else"—by which I mean something outside of, external to, different from, inexplicable in terms of the logic of cause and effect—what I'm really saying is that there is something outside of, external to, different from, inexplicable in terms of the logic of cause and effect that is, at the same time, inside of, internal to, an integral part of and explicable in terms of the logic of cause and effect—which, of course, is nonsense.

I cannot talk about something—anything, by which I mean any thing—without bringing it under the categories of cause and effect. Language—the language of thing-ness—just won't let me do it. Try as I might, I am utterly, completely, and eternally unable to find words and sentences to express what I have in mind. It's impossible for me to articulate in language—not just the English language, but any language with which I'm familiar—the idea of something, some thing, that exists outside of the logic of cause and effect. Because if it's some thing, it exists, and if it exists, it must have been caused to exist by something other than itself, and so on ad infinitum.

But don't blame language. Poor old language, after all, is just the reflection of, the bearer of, the outward manifestation of, our ideas. The real culprit is thought. Human thought (of which language, to be sure, is an inextricable part). The fact that language cannot express the idea of Something Else—of something existing outside the structure of cause and effect—is simply and solely a result of the fact that we cannot really have that thought. We cannot have that idea. It looks like an idea, but it's not. There's no idea there.

And yet . . .

And yet the world exists. There must be an explanation. The logic of cause and effect can't explain it. So I want to say there must be Something Else.

But as we've just seen, I can't say that. Not allowed. Forbidden. Out of bounds.

So I'm stuck. We're stuck.

Now when I was talking about Something Else—which I'm not going to do any more, because that was a mistake—wasn't I just doing what lots of theists are doing when they claim there must be a God even if they can't know who or what God is?

Actually, I wasn't.

There's a huge difference between Something Else and God. The idea of God is the idea of a First Thing, an Unmoved Mover, an all-powerful creature or entity who has created everything else but who is Himself (or Herself or Itself) uncreated. And clearly such an idea is totally, entirely, and completely *within*, not outside of, the logic of cause and effect. Indeed, it's precisely the logic of cause and effect—the idea that there must have been something that started everything else—that gave rise to the idea in the first place. Of course, just as the logic of cause and effect gave rise to the idea, so it also destroys the idea, since if there was a First Thing, then it must have been caused by something other than itself, in which case it wasn't the First Thing at all, and so on ad infinitum. And so what seemed like an idea turns out not be an idea at all.

The idea of Something Else is also not an idea. But here the problem isn't that when I was talking about Something Else, I wasn't talking about something that both cannot exist and must exist at the same time. The problem here is different. The problem is that language won't let me express what I want to express. It won't let me say what I want to say. In fact, on this particular topic, it won't let me say anything at all. Nothing. Not one single word. Nada. Zero. Zilch.

What I want to do is talk about something that exists completely apart from the logic of cause and effect. But oops! Look! Right there! Hold the presses! I've just done what I can't do. I've just used the phrase "something that exists." And the second—the very instant—I do that, I'm talking about cause and effect. I'm talking about a thing; and if it's a thing, it exists; and if it exists, it must have been caused. Now I don't want to do that. I want entirely to avoid the logic of cause and effect. I want to speak in a completely different way. I want to talk about something that does *not* involve cause and effect. I want—but ouch! Stop! There! Right there! I've done it again! "Something." I've just used that word. Of course, this time I didn't use the whole phrase "something that exists." But no matter. Because when I use the word *something*, I'm talking about—here we go—a thing, which, if it's a thing, must exist, and which, if it exists, must have been caused.

And yet . . .

And yet the world exists. There *has* to be an explanation. The logic of cause and effect can't explain it. So what I want to say—which I cannot and will not say, ever again, I promise, because it doesn't make any sense and because language won't allow it—what I want to say is that there *must be* Something Else.

Not a First Thing. We know that's impossible. Not an Unmoved Mover. Huh? Not an all-powerful creator. Makes no sense. Not God. No such idea.

But Something Else.

Which I cannot say.

So I'll say something else. Not Something Else, but something else. And here's what I'll say:

This—by which I mean the world of cause and effect, the world as we know it, the only world we could ever know, the only world that's conceptually possible—this can't be all there is.

So what I'm doing now is proposing to avoid the problem of Something Else by formulating things in purely negative terms. Instead of saying—positively—there must be Something

Else, I'll just stick with the negative claim: this—the world of cause and effect—can't be all there is. It can't be the whole story. The idea that the world is simply and solely a world of cause and effect provides a grotesquely impoverished view of things. It purports to offer an adequate explanation of the world, but it fails. Miserably. It's inaccurate, misleading, and just plain wrong. It is, above all, radically and massively incomplete. So I'm trying to state my idea without making any assertions at all about "things" and "existence" or anything else—assertions that would necessarily trigger the logic of cause and effect.

But let's be honest. This doesn't work either. It doesn't work because all of those negative phrases necessarily and unavoidably imply the positive stuff. Can't get away from it.

There's a very important theory in philosophy called speech-act theory. The details can be pretty complicated, but the basic point is actually quite simple. When we say things, we're very often expressing thoughts that are not actually expressed by the literal meaning of the words themselves. I call you on the phone and say "Is Trixie there?" Think about the literal meaning of that question. It simply asks you to provide me with a fact, namely, whether or not Trixie is there. Is it true that, at this particular time, Trixie is in that particular space? That's the literal meaning—the entire literal meaning—of the words I've uttered. Nothing else. But most of the time, when I utter those words I'm really saying something quite different. I'm not only asking the factual question about whether or not Trixie's there. I'm also asking you to call her to the phone. I didn't actually use the words "would you call Trixie to the phone," but most of the time that's certainly what my utterance means. The literal meaning of my words doesn't fully capture the actual meaning of my speech-act. Another example: we're at the dinner table and I say "Could you pass the salt?" Again, according to the strictly literal meaning of my words, I'm simply asking a factual question: are you able to pass the salt? Is this something that you have the ability to do? But most of the time, we know I'm really saying something very, very different. I already know darn well that you have the ability to pass the salt. I don't need to ask about that. But what I want is the salt. So pass it. Please. Literal meaning and what might be called functional meaning are two different things.

And that's the problem with my purely negative solution. Because when I say "this can't be all there is," I'm necessarily implying—I'm in effect saying—that there's Something Else. That's what it means to say "this can't be all there is." When I say that "it can't be the whole story," I'm necessarily saying that there is—there exists—Something Else that would make the story whole. When I say "it's incomplete," I can't help but communicate the view—the positive view—that things are, in fact, complete, but only because of Something Else.[3]

Of course, if I try to talk about Something Else, I'm trying to talk about something that exists completely apart from the logic of cause and effect. But Geez! Hold it! There I go again! "Something that exists . . . " Can't say that!

Can't say anything!

And ultimately, that's exactly right. Can't say anything. Because in this case, language makes it completely and entirely impossible for me to express what I want to express. And again, it's not the fault of language. In fact, language—not just literal language, as we've seen, but language in the fullest sense of the word—language is a pretty good test. Thought and language are really just two sides of the very same coin. No thoughts without language, no language without thoughts. Which means that if I can't express an idea in language, then there's probably no idea to express. And so I think I have an idea, the idea of Something Else. This is not the idea of God, of a First Thing, of an Unmoved Mover. It's totally different. It's the idea of something existing outside the logic of cause and effect. But even though I think I have the idea, I really don't. There's no idea there. No idea to express.

So I need to do one thing and one thing only, and that's to keep my mouth shut. I need to say nothing. I mean it. Nada. Zero. Zilch.

And yet . . .

And yet the world exists. There *must* be an explanation. The logic of cause and effect can't explain it. So there must be . . . Well, language cannot express it. Indeed, there's no "it" to be expressed, since any *it* would involve a something, and that something would exist, and there we go again. So language cannot express it. And if language cannot express it, that means we cannot think it. There is no thought there—no concept, no notion, no idea.

The resources of human thought are far too paltry, far too pitiful, to have any such idea. The hopeless inadequacy of the human mind—that's what we're faced with. And that's what we're stuck with, forever. You see, it's a kind of a prison—the prison of the logic of cause and effect, the prison of the human intellect. That's our prison, our jail, our penitentiary, our pokey, our slammer, our hoosegow, our stir. We're stuck in it and we can never get out of it. Never. Of course, it's not all bad. In fact, as jails go, it's actually a pretty terrific place. Just think of who is inside the prison with us. Think of our fellow inmates. Plato. Thomas Aquinas. Kant.

Virgil and Dante and Shakespeare. Dostoevsky and Dickens, Joyce and (my own personal favorite) Conrad. Raphael and Caravaggio and Claude Monet. Newton and Leibniz, tending to the calculus; Darwin, contemplating his theory of evolution; Watson and Crick, brandishing their double helix. Mozart, Beethoven, Brahms. Charlie Parker![4] And so on and so on, ad infinitum. Only this time it's a good ad infinitum. A wonderful ad infinitum. A great ad infinitum. Brings tears to my eyes just thinking about it.

But as far as the world itself is concerned, as far as really explaining the universe, where it came from, what it all means—nothing. Hopeless. As far as all this is concerned, the prison is a dungeon.

The world exists. There must be an explanation. But—and if I don't break the rule, I can't write a sentence, any sentence, so here goes—the explanation must be something utterly foreign to, completely different from, entirely alien to the basic structure of human thought, something completely outside the category of "something," something that's not a "something" at all, something that doesn't "exist," that has no characteristics, no features, no traits, no movement, no location—all of which doesn't make any sense but which nonetheless must be true.

In other words: This—the world of cause and effect, the world as we know it, the only world we could ever know, the only world that's conceptually possible—this can't be all there is.

And that's the good news. In fact, it's great news.

Because what it means, I think, is that we cannot be utterly and entirely alone. Clear away all the God-talk—all the mumbo-jumbo about proving and disproving and doubting the existence of a First Thing or an Unmoved Mover, all the dead-end chatter about something that absolutely cannot exist and absolutely must exist at the same time—get rid of all that and what's left?

What's left is that the universe—the real universe—cannot possibly be just a bunch of meaningless material stuff. It's impossible that there's nothing but atoms and molecules and other hunks of matter, just clanking around. It's impossible—literally impossible, as a matter of demonstrable fact—that the world is simply a matter of physical cause and effect. That just cannot be.

The world exists. But it's simply impossible that this—the world of cause and effect, our world of cause and effect, the world that we know and understand, the world that is completely and totally and eternally incapable of explaining how the world came into existence—it's impossible that this is all there is. Utterly and entirely impossible. Of course, there I go one more time, trying to express the inexpressible. Pretending I have an idea when I really don't. I'm sorry. I won't do it again. I won't say another word. Except to say—lamely, incoherently, as quietly as possible, in a whisper—that this cannot be all there is. That if the pathetic limits of the human mind cannot be transcended—which they cannot—there nonetheless absolutely must be something (*sic!!*) that is indeed transcendent. I hope you can see that this is not a matter of faith. It's not a guess. It's not a wish. It's simply and completely and undeniably true.

And that makes the world seem a little less bleak, doesn't it? A little less lonely? A little less empty? Maybe even a lot less empty? The notion that this—the system of cause and effect—simply can't be all there is? That there must be, okay not Something Else, but something . . . more? Or transcendent? Or different? Or . . . well, let's just say something that's not really something at all but that's nonetheless—and, obviously, for lack of a better word—s-o-m-e-t-h-i-n-g . . . ?

Enough said.

In fact, I've already said far too much.

I've said things I know I can't say. I've expressed ideas that can't be expressed because they're not really ideas at all. So I'll stop now. I'll keep quiet. I won't say another word. I promise.

Except to say that I think all of this is actually going to help me with the willies. Indeed, it cheers me up. It cheers me up lot. A whole lot.

In fact, I'm actually feeling pretty good about things right now.

You?

AFTERWORD: NOT ENOUGH?

Would you like to read some more? The literature is beyond huge. It's absolutely mammoth. At least some of it is really, really interesting—often brilliant—but far beyond what most readers of this book will want to take on. Here, however, is a tiny handful of high-quality items that would provide a more extensive introduction to at least some of the things I've been talking about.

A good place to begin would be Aristotle himself, specifically, Book Lambda (or "L") of his *Metaphysics*. That's where we encounter, I believe for the very first time, the notion of an Unmoved Mover—which means that the notion is more than 2,300 years old.

A classic statement of the claim that "nothing comes from nothing" was provided by Lucretius in his extremely important and really amazingly impressive work, *On the Nature of Things*. This is a philosophical poem of ancient Rome, written (in epic meter) during the first century BCE. Lucretius was an Epicurean—by which we mean not a lover of fine food but a follower of the philosophy of Epicurus. He—Lucretius—was a kind of "atomist." Like us, he believed that the world is basically composed of atoms. He also believed that the world was originally created not by the gods but by the mixing up and combination of atoms, perhaps a kind of proto–Big Bang. Lucretius wasn't too crazy about religion. In fact, he hated it. But it's perhaps notable that his great poem does begin with an invocation to the goddess Venus. Not sure what to make of that.

For a canonical statement of the cosmological argument within the Abrahamic—that is, the Judeo-Christian-Islamic—tradition, see Thomas Aquinas's *Summa Theologica*, First Part, Question 2, Article 3. It's there that we actually find Thomas's famous five arguments for—or "five ways" to prove—the existence of God. The five ways include the ontological argument and the so-called argument from design as well as the cosmological argument. For an extremely important and deeply intelligent criticism of St. Thomas, you should look at Anthony Kenney's *The Five Ways*, a wonderful book.

Another canonical version of the cosmological argument, this time coming from modern England, is to be found in John Locke's *Essay Concerning Human Understanding*, especially in Book IV, Chapter 10, Sections 1–3. Locke actually makes for pretty easy reading, and you don't have to devour the whole book to get this particular part of it. Like Thomas, however, his argument for the existence of God isn't limited to the cosmological argument. Both of them adopt a full-court-press—or kitchen sink—strategy.

In his *Dialogues on Natural Religion*, especially Part IX, David Hume, the great eighteenth-century Scottish philosopher, denies that there's anything contradictory in believing that some of the things that exist were not caused to exist. He seems to reject, in other words, the necessity of the logic of cause and effect. Note, however, that my presentation is an attempt to reconstruct the nature of ordinary thinking—what makes sense for ordinary people like you and me to believe—and that's not quite the same as attempting to prove what's logically possible and impossible. Or is it?

Presumably the next person to cite would be Kant, whom I've referred to several times. Kant, however, raises a different set of problems. So let me put that off for a moment. Bear with me.

Of more recent books, I've already mentioned (note 6 in chapter 2) J. L. Mackie's *The Miracle of Belief*, which is really just terrific and also quite accessible. Mackie was an atheist—not so much because he thought he had proven that God doesn't exist but because he believed, all in all, that God's non-existence is more likely to be true.

Perhaps especially prominent among the comparatively few academic philosophers who seem actually to believe in God is Alvin Plantinga. Plantinga is a prolific author, and much of what he has written is for a strictly academic audience. But I'd recommend a wonderful essay entitled "Reason and Belief in God," which is in a book called *The Analytic Theist* and is quite readable. In this essay, Plantinga acknowledges that some versions of the kind of argument I've been trying to make here might actually be "of great interest." He nonetheless insists, like Mackie, that the concept of God is perfectly coherent. Also like Mackie, he frustratingly fails to say why; and like Mackie again, he frustratingly fails to cite any literature. Now if Plantinga were to read my book, it's pretty clear he'd hate it, but the feeling wouldn't be mutual. This is a very serious guy, and I wouldn't want to meet him in the philosophical equivalent of a dark alley (unless the weapons of choice, so to speak, were political rather religious).

I'm also much taken with a book by Bede Rundle entitled *Why There Is Something Rather Than Nothing*. Perhaps I like it because I agree with much (though not all) of it. For example, when Rundle says "I can get no grip on the idea of an agent doing something where the doing, the bringing about, is not an episode in time," I find myself precisely as grip-less as he does, and for pretty much the same reasons. Similarly, the idea of a First Cause makes as little sense to Rundle as it does to me. And when he says that scientists—like Big Bang theorists or Higgs particle theorists—"have something to say only once their subject matter, the physical universe, is supposed in being," this seems to me exactly right.

But for a fairly sophisticated account—and defense—of some of the scientifically informed views that Rundle criticizes, I'd recommend William Lane Craig and Quentin Smith, *Theism, Atheism, and Big Bang Cosmology*. Craig defends theism and Smith atheism—both in the context of (what I take to be) a serious understanding of the physics and mathematics of Big Bang theory.

And now for Kant—last but very far from least. Ideally, of all the writers you should look at, he's the most important. In fact, I might suggest, without too much exaggeration, that pretty much all of Western philosophy after Kant is largely an attempt to come to grips with—to refute or refine or reinterpret or reanimate—Kant's system of thought. And this is probably true not only of his thought in general but of his thought about God. Now to at least some extent Kant's philosophy was written as a systematic criticism of none other than David Hume. Among many other things, Kant insists on the ubiquity of the logic of cause and effect, and I'll have more to say about that in a moment. But as to the question of God itself, Kant provides powerful and extremely influential criticisms of both the cosmological and ontological arguments. See, primarily, Book II, Chapter III of the Second Division of the Second Part of the *Critique of Pure Reason*—which I myself believe to be the most important philosophical work of the modern age.

The problem with Kant, however—and what distinguishes him even from great writers such as Aristotle and Hume—is not only that he's very, very tough to read, though he is. The problem is it doesn't make a whole lot of sense to read just a little bit of Kant. Because if you try to read just a little bit of Kant, you really won't have the slightest idea of what he's talking about. To know what he's talking about, you need to read a great deal of Kant; and reading any Kant at all, much less lots and lots of Kant, is, it must be said, an awfully tall order. Interestingly, Kant himself realized this. He recognized that his writings were extremely difficult. Indeed, during his own lifetime, critics attacked his books for being nearly indecipherable, and he himself never denied the criticism. So at one point he decided to write a couple of books—actually quite short books—that were designed to summarize his ideas for the average undergrad and the average reader, like you and me. You might say he wrote his own Monarch Notes. Short little introductions to his work. Kant-Made-Simple. And written by Kant himself, straight from the horse's mouth. One of these books is called *Prolegomena to Any Future Metaphysics*, the other *Foundations of the Metaphysics of Morals*. If you think those are daunting titles, you're right. But it's not just the titles that are daunting; it's the books themselves. What Kant considered easy and simple is, for ordinary humans like many of you and certainly for me, far from it. In fact, these two nice little books are killers. The *Prolegomena* in particular is not the kind of book you'd want to pick up and take to the beach on a sunny day.

And yet, as I say, Kant is really important. I can't recommend that you just read a few sections of Kant, but I can't just let it go either. So let me talk a little bit about Kant's thought here as a kind of brief substitute for beach reading. Consider this a (hopefully) useful if (unfortunately) overly simplistic primer, designed not so much to whet your appetite as to take the edge off it, at least for a while. Let's call it Kant-Made-Simple-Made-Simple.

Now in some ways the most interesting thing about Kant himself—Kant the man—is how massively uninteresting he was. I should say that this has actually been somewhat exaggerated over the years by the mythmakers, who make him out to be boring beyond belief. In fact, evidence suggests that he was actually a very fine person, a very popular teacher, a pleasant and engaging fellow, the soul of good common sense. He never married, but he liked to socialize well enough and had plenty of friends. So we're not talking about Mr. Spock or someone out of Dilbert. Nonetheless, there's an absolutely astonishing, indeed mind-boggling fact about Kant. He lived in Königsberg—which was the capital of East Prussia in those days, and which was a reasonably important city, though hardly a great city. Today, by the way, Königsberg is in Russia—actually it's in a part of Russia that's geographically unconnected with any other part of Russia—and it's not called Königsberg. It's called Kaliningrad. But that's not the astonishing fact. The astonishing fact is that Kant never left Königsberg. And when I say never, I mean never. Really never. I don't simply mean he lived there his whole life, though he did. I mean he never set foot anywhere else. Here's a gentleman who was, for a while, a well-known and quite popular author of philosophical and scientific books and who, after another while, became a world-famous author of philosophical and scientific books, maybe the most famous author of all. Here's also a fellow who lived to be eighty (1724–1804). And in eighty years on this earth, this world-famous and enormously influential writer never—not even once—wandered more than ten miles from Königsberg. He never even went to Vilnius or Warsaw or Stockholm, all pretty close, much less to Berlin or Munich or Vienna. Paris and London and Rome? No way. In his entire life, he never once went to an out-of-town conference or colloquium, never gave a lecture at another university, never visited the home of a fellow great thinker, never traveled to receive an award or honorary degree. He also never enjoyed what most of us would think of as a real vacation. He never went to a spa to take the waters, never went to the Riviera to soak up some rays, never hiked the Black Forest. Here's a European of extraordinary learning and culture, an internationally renowned intellectual, a person of massive and astonishing erudition, who never saw—and presumably had no desire ever to see—an Alp. Never saw the Atlantic or the Mediterranean. Never saw the Rhine or the Danube. Never ate French pastry or Italian pasta—at least not in France or Italy. The Parthenon? The Forum? St. Peter's? Nope. No interest, I guess.

This would be like someone today who's the greatest thinker in the world—someone upon whom the world has lavished praise, whose books are read by millions, who's a sensible and engaging fellow, who likes to party as much as the next guy—but who has not only decided to live his entire life in, say, Omaha, but who has never ever left the State of Nebraska, not even once, except perhaps to have a burger in Council Bluffs. Not even St. Louis or Kansas City, for God's sake.

Kant was a late-bloomer. He was a prof at the University of—where else?—Königsberg, and had a pretty good career going, writing a lot about things like astronomy. He had, as we say today in the world of higher ed, a very decent publication record. Nothing earth-shattering, but solid. Even excellent. But then, at the age of forty-six, something happened. I myself think he had an epiphany—undoubtedly sitting in his carriage on the corner of, perhaps, Friedrichstrasse and Leipzigerstrasse in downtown Königsberg, waiting for the traffic to pass. He had read David Hume and, suddenly, something about Hume hit him like a ton of bricks. Right there. In Königsberg. A ton of bricks.

For about ten years he didn't publish a single word. And for about ten years, he holed himself up pretty well. Not so many parties. Immanuel Kant had his epiphany and then spent about ten years working it out. But work it out he did. And finally, out came a torrent of words—difficult words to read, yes, but really important words nonetheless. A couple thousand pages' worth. So the Kant we now know and love didn't actually emerge until he himself was almost sixty. Which means there's hope for all of us. (Well, most of us. I'm already over sixty, so it's too late for me.)

Now David Hume was very interested in the question of causation. I assume his local department store, unlike mine, had a billiards table rather than dominoes, because when it came to causation, billiards was his thing. If you've read note 1 in chapter 1, you know the drill: you hit the cue ball into the three ball, the three ball then hits the six ball and the six ball bangs into the four ball, the four ball caroms off the cushion before kissing the eight ball, knocking it—the eight ball—into the side pocket. At each individual point, one ball causes the next ball to move. The cue ball hitting the three ball causes the three ball to move until it hits the six ball, and so on. A causal chain. Seems commonsensical. But Hume has something interesting to say about this.

Hume believed that pretty much every idea we have—every thought that pops into your head or my head—is really a reflection or image of something that we've seen with our eyes or otherwise observed with our senses. You have the idea of a dog in your head. But there's only one reason why you have the idea of a dog, and that's because you've actually seen a dog with your eyes. If you've never seen a dog, the idea of a dog would never have occurred to you. All of our ideas are, in other words, based on sense-perception. Of course, it's true that we also have the idea of a unicorn, even though we've never seen a unicorn. But Hume says that's easy to explain. While all of our ideas are images and are based on things we've actually observed with our senses, we also have imaginations. And that means that we can imagine combining some of the ideas or images that are in our heads. In that way, we can imagine—we can form—a kind of composite idea. We've never seen a unicorn. But we have seen horses and we have seen horns, so all we have to do is use our imagination to combine the image of a horse with the image of a horn and, presto, we have the idea of a unicorn. A composite idea. If we had seen a horse but had never, ever seen a horn, we couldn't have the idea of unicorn. Our imagination allows us to compose or invent all kinds of ideas or images, but only provided those ideas or images are composed of ideas or images of things that we've actually seen with our eyes or otherwise observed with our senses.

What does that have to do with billiard balls? Well, Hume says that when we watch the billiard balls move, that's really all we see. The only thing we see is the motion—in time—of the billiard balls themselves. The physical motion of the physical things. First we see the motion of the cue ball. We see it rolling across the table. Then we see it hitting the three ball. Then we see the motion of the three ball across the table. And so on. That's it. We don't see anything else. And if we don't see anything else, we don't have an image of anything else. In particular—and here's the punch line—we don't see, hence don't have an image of, the cause. If all of our ideas are limited to things we actually observe, and if all we actually observe are the individual motions of the balls themselves, then we really don't haven't any idea, deep down, of what causes the balls to move. We don't observe the cause itself. And if that's the punch line, then here's the payoff: the notion that one billiard ball causes the other billiard ball to move is nothing but a figment of our imagination. It's like the unicorn. We watch the sequential motion of the billiards balls—the one hitting the other, which then hits the next, which then, in turn, hits the next, and so on—and we imagine that what we're seeing is a process of physical causation, a causal chain. We use the imagination to put together the images of the balls moving, and thereby we produce a composite idea, the idea of each ball causing the next one to move. But since we never actually see the cause—we only see the separate individual motions of the balls—this is just something we've made up. We've invented it. It's a fiction. Just like a unicorn.

Now Hume is at pains to add this very important point: the fiction of physical causation—the fiction that the one billiard ball causes the next billiard ball to move, and so on—is, unlike the unicorn, a really, really useful fiction. It's a fiction that allows us to live in the world. It's a fiction that actually allows us to play billiards. After all, if we didn't imagine a causal chain among billiard balls, playing billiards would be silly, even unthinkable. The idea of causal chains is a fiction that allows us to build buildings and to play baseball and to cook food. It's a fiction that allows us to do science. It's a fiction that makes it possible for us to make plans and to live productive lives. So it's an absolutely terrific fiction. But a fiction nonetheless. There is, says Hume, nothing in our observations that would deny the possibility that the billiard balls are not really causing each other to move. It's possible, for example, that each billiard ball is really at the end of an invisible string controlled by an evil demon who is playing with our minds, making the billiard balls move in an orderly fashion, encouraging us to get used to the balls moving in an orderly fashion, encouraging us to believe that one is causing the other to move, and just waiting to mess us up by, next time, deciding not to move the balls at all.

So now Kant is thinking about Hume and nodding his head, sitting there at the corner of Friedrichstrasse and Leipzigerstrasse, but then something hits him. Like a ton of bricks. If Hume's basic point is right—in particular, if it's true that all of our ideas are either images of things we've actually seen or imagined composites of the image of things we've actually seen—then this leaves a basic question unanswered: where did the idea of cause itself come from? Because the idea of cause is, in fact, not like the idea of unicorn. This is where Hume messed up, at least according to Kant (and for what it's worth, I think Kant's right). A unicorn is the imagined composite of two things we've observed, a horse and horn. Combine those two images in our mind and we can imagine a unicorn, even though we've never seen one. But if you combine the image of the motion of the cue ball and the image of the motion of the three ball, all you get is an image of two balls moving at different points in time and space, first the one, then the other. And from that composite image, you don't get any notion of causality. Why would you? Let me repeat this: if all of our ideas are reflections of things we've seen and observed, and if we see and observe some billiard balls moving, then there's no reason to have the idea of causation, because if you put the motion of two billiard balls together all you get is the motion of two billiard balls together, you don't get cause. The idea of a cause is, you see, brand new. It's different. It's something that's been added on. It's not reducible to any combination of images of things. It's an idea that is separate from—an idea that's in addition to—the images of the motion of the billiard balls.

And that's a problem. Because if it's true that all of our ideas are images of things that we've seen and observed, or composites of images of things that we've seen and observed, then it's actually impossible that we could ever have the idea of a cause—since we've never actually seen or observed a cause. That's a problem because in fact we do have the idea of a cause. Nothing could be more obvious. Can't deny it. Again, that's why we can play billiards. And do science. And make plans. Indeed, if we didn't have the idea of cause, I couldn't have written this paragraph and you couldn't have read it. Or at least you couldn't have made any sense of it. So the $64,000 question: where does the idea of cause come from?

Kant says there's only one possibility: not all of our ideas are images of things that we've seen and observed or composites of images of things that we've seen and observed. We have no choice, says Kant, but to conclude that we actually have ideas—that our brains have conceptual tools—that exist on their own, separate from and prior to our observations of things in the world. We don't get the idea of causation from our observations. We already have the idea of causation. That idea must be inherent in us. We're born with it. It must be part of the way our minds operate. And so when we observe things—when we see the billiard balls—we simply apply our own idea of causation to what we observe and, voila, we can play billiards.

Here, then, is a revolution. Kant himself thought it was equivalent to the Copernican Revolution, whereby Copernicus discovered that the earth revolves around the sun, not vice versa. In Kant's case, he discovered what absolutely must be true, namely, that our minds—our ideas and thoughts—are not simply and solely reflections of the world out there but that, to the contrary, when we observe and think about the world out there our minds are actually arranging and ordering the things we see. We impose a structure on things. That doesn't mean we create reality. But it does mean that everything we take to be real is, at least in part, a result of how we interpret the things we see. So when you're walking down the street or on the Riviera or in the Alps or wherever and you're looking around you, absorbing all the sights and sounds and feels, you're mind is not really a passive receptacle of sense impressions. It's actively imposing a kind of intellectual structure—a structure of thought—on everything you experience.

Now for reasons that are too complicated to go into here, Kant thinks that causation is not the only idea that we have inherently. In fact, he thinks that lots of our ideas are ideas that are not in any way reducible to images of things we have observed. Among these are very basic ideas (actually Kant calls them intuitions) of space and time itself. The reason for this is that from the simple physical observation of the billiard balls—the physical act of sensing with your eyes those balls moving around the table—you can't get the notion of things happening in space or time. That's a difficult claim, but think about it this way. Imagine an amoeba. Imagine what is probably true, that an amoeba has a sensory apparatus. Of course, its apparatus is much simpler than ours. All it can do, we might say, is feel things. But feeling is a matter of sensation. If an amoeba gets poked, say by another amoeba, it moves. It moves, one might guess, because it feels the poke. It senses the poke. So amoebae have sense. But imagine now that the amoeba gets poked again—a second poke. Now what could this possibly mean—so to speak—to the amoeba? Remember, amoebae are really, really dumb. All they can do is feel pokes. Pure sense impressions. So from the perspective of the amoeba, there's no connection between the first poke and the second. They're just pokes—random, independent, unrelated. The amoeba does not have an intellectual structure—intuitions of space and time—on the basis of which to relate the one poke to the other. And without such a structure, there's no order, no rhyme or reason, to the pokes. The amoeba has no sense of here or there, of now and then. The amoeba doesn't know, for example, that the first poke came first and the second poke came later. The amoeba doesn't have an idea of time. We, on the other hand, are not amoebae. When we get poked and poked again, we know that one poke was here and the other was there. In another words, we can place the pokes, relative to one another, in space. And we know that one poke was then and the other was now. In other words, we can place the pokes, relative to one another, in time. But none of that is possible if all we have—if all our ideas are completely and entirely reducible to—the feelings of the pokes themselves. We ourselves must bring to the pokes a massive intellectual structure that includes such things as space, time, and causation, an intellectual structure that we can't get from pure feels themselves but that must simply be part of how the human mind operates.

So that, in a tiny nutshell, was Kant's epiphany. And as I say, it's an epiphany that has set the agenda for virtually all philosophy since then, which means virtually all philosophy of the last two hundred years. It also sets the agenda for Kant's own thinking about God. Now as I've mentioned above, Kant is most famous for his severe criticisms of both the cosmological and ontological arguments for the existence of God; and as I've mentioned before, I'm hesitant to recommend that you look at the relevant sections of the *Critique of Pure Reason*. But late in life, Kant did write a book devoted entirely to the question of God itself, a really interesting book that's difficult but not nearly as difficult as the *Critique of Pure Reason* and that you actually might want to dip your toes into. It's called *Religion Within the Bounds of Reason Alone*. And it's there that Kant claims both that it is and will always be impossible—indeed, silly—to try to prove either the existence or non-existence of God but that, despite this, it's nonetheless really important to have religion. As you might guess, I agree with the first part of this and can't for the life of me see how the second part could possibly be right. But he's Kant and I'm only me, and who am I to criticize him? In any case, you might want to see for yourself. If you do, and if you figure out how Kant's right and how I'm wrong—if you have your own epiphany—let me know. I mean that seriously. I'd be interested.

So those are some of my recommendations for additional reading. I've actually given you a pretty fair amount. But if you want much more than this, it's probably time to begin thinking about grad school. And God knows, there are a lot worse things you could be thinking about!

AMPLIFICATIONS AND CLARIFICATIONS (AKA NOTES)

1. THE PROBLEM WITH GOD

1. Yes, a dreaded footnote! Or, rather, a dreaded backnote. Or so it might appear. In a work of traditional scholarship, of course, notes are really important. They refer to, and sometimes describe, what other scholars have written about the same subject. But the book you're now reading is not a work of traditional scholarship, and so there's no need for traditional notes. Every so often, however, I'll need to throw in a note, in part to keep the critics (somewhat) at bay, and in part just to amplify or clarify or otherwise expand on some point I've made, and to do so without interrupting the flow, as we say, of the narrative. I promise to keep these to a minimum.

   So here you should know, if you don't already, that the dominoes metaphor is hardly unique to me. In fact, it's almost ubiquitous, not just in discussions of geopolitics—we fought the

Vietnam War at least in part because of the domino theory—but in discussions of causation as well. The reason is simple: it's just a very good image of a causal chain. Of course, another good image is billiards. You hit the cue ball into the three ball, the three ball then hits the six ball and the six ball bangs into the four ball, the four ball caroms off the cushion before kissing the eight ball, knocking it—the eight ball—into the side pocket. Which means, if you happen to be playing a game of eight ball and provided you've already knocked in all the other solid balls, you win. I know: that's not billiards, that's pool. But you get the idea. A causal chain. The only problem with this image is that, as far as I can remember, my old department store didn't have a pool table. Hence, dominoes.

2. I promised to keep these notes to a minimum, and I will. But in the present case, I've just said that the argument for God "goes roughly as follows." The truth, however, is that there are lots and lots of arguments for God and I'm really only dealing with one of them. The one I'm dealing with is often called the "cosmological argument." I do think it's by far the best argument for the existence of God—though I also think it's an argument that just doesn't work. It is, let us say, the least bad argument. But historically, an equally famous and influential argument for the existence of God is called the "ontological argument." It's generally attributed, first, to St. Anselm, who was the Archbishop of Canterbury around the turn of the twelfth century and was one of the very first of the so-called "scholastic" thinkers of the Middle Ages; and, later, to René Descartes, the great French philosopher of the seventeenth century. Now I shall have nothing to say here about this argument, and there are very good reasons for that. In the late eighteenth century, Immanuel Kant—the

greatest philosopher by far of the modern age—wrote a book called *The Critique of Pure Reason.* I don't recommend you read it, unless you have about two years to kill. But you should know that a relatively small part of the *Critique* is devoted to the ontological argument, and Kant absolutely demolishes it. Smashes it to smithereens. Since then, relatively few people have taken the argument very seriously, though there are still some diehards out there. In any case, I'm going to ignore it, and you can be pretty confident that you're not missing anything you desperately need.

3. In emphasizing faith, I think I'm agreeing with the great Austrian philosopher of the twentieth century, Ludwig Wittgenstein. In his "Lectures on Religious Belief," Wittgenstein seems to say that claims about God are just different from other kinds of claims, and that the difference is largely a matter of whether or not faith comes into play. God-claims are faith-based; other, more ordinary claims are evidence-based. Now I must confess that I'm not 100 percent sure I've got this right. Wittgenstein's lectures—which he never wrote or published, but which have been compiled from notes taken by three of his students—are easy to read but not so easy to understand. Nonetheless, I think I'm pretty close.

   It may be that another version of the same general view—the view that religion is basically a matter of faith—can be found in the work of the important contemporary French philosopher Jean-Luc Marion. But again, I'm not entirely sure. Marion's writings are not only difficult to understand; they're darned difficult to read.

4. At the very same time, however, Bacon also condemned "superstition." Just how he distinguished faith in "incredible" things from superstition is—you should pardon the expression (see chapter 9)—a mystery.

5. The sharp-eyed among you may have already noticed that I've been playing a bit fast and loose with such notions as concept, thought, and image. The fact is that these are different things. A thought is, roughly speaking, something that the mind produces. As such, any particular thought might reflect, invoke, or rely upon one or more concepts. But to reflect, invoke, or rely upon a concept is not the same as actually being a concept. Similarly, an image—in the context of the present discussion—is a kind of mental picture, something produced by the faculty of the imagination; and an image might be the (imagined) picture of a concept. But again, an image of something is not the same as the thing itself, any more than a painting of a chair is the same as a real chair. So yes, all of these things should be kept separate, strictly speaking. But notice: an impossible concept—a concept that simply does not exist—cannot give rise to a thought, since there's nothing to reflect, invoke, or rely upon. Nor can it provide the basis for an image, since there's nothing to picture. Thus, the impossibility of thinking about or picturing a First Cause that is, at the same time, not a First Cause is, in and of itself, important evidence for the impossibility of such a concept. The upshot is that, for our purposes, differences among concept, thought, and image are nothing to get too excited about.

   Now, the fact is that I could write a couple more paragraphs—or, indeed, a couple more pages—justifying, or at least attempting to justify, what I've just said. And frankly, such an exercise could be repeated many times over in this book. But I won't do that, because if I did, the result would be to change the character of the book dramatically. It would become a different book, something written for professional philosophers rather than general readers, and that would completely defeat the purpose. Of course, it's true that my goal has been, in part, to speak to general readers in a way that respects, to the degree possible, the terminological and conceptual exigencies of philosophical analysis, which I take very seriously. But in doing the actual writing, I've found that to be a pretty difficult goal to achieve. Impossible, in fact—though I should add, for any philosophers out there who might be reading this, that if you feel you could have done it better than I have, more power to you. I mean that sincerely. All I can say is, I've tried my best.

2. WHAT IN GOD'S NAME AM I DOING?

1. In actual fact, I think I really am doing a certain kind of metaphysics, but my understanding of that word is rather different from how it was understood for about twenty centuries. I'm doing what's sometimes called "descriptive metaphysics." I'm not describing how things in the world really are. Rather, I'm describing our thoughts about how things in the world really are.
2. An obscure allusion to a truly great, if largely unheralded, movie, Preston Sturges' *Hail the Conquering Hero* (1944). In a fit of manic frustration, our protagonist, Woodrow Truesmith, turns to Marine Corporal Walewski—a sweet, simple, but fiercely principled human being who also happens to have a screw loose—and says, "What, are you crazy?" To which Walewski, without missing a beat, responds deadpan: "Mebbe." This flick, I should say, is a work of genius—a work of *philosophical* genius—that unearths and brings to light our own shared, underlying, innermost beliefs about war and peace, politics and love, truth and illusion, cause and effect. It also just might be, believe it or not, the best comedy ever made, though its greatness has gone largely unrecognized. If you haven't seen it, check it out.

3. Of course, Bonds was convicted, in March 2011, of one count of obstruction of justice. But that's not the same thing.
4. In general, women play softball, not baseball. But there are exceptions. Remember *A League of Their Own* (1992), the movie with Tom Hanks and Geena Davis?
5. And to the degree that all philosophy really is a matter of rationally reconstructing our ordinary thoughts, this problem—the problem of saying something truly new—is a problem not just for me but for philosophers in general. If you want to read a bit more about this, you might want to look at Wittgenstein's *Philosophical Investigations*—despite appearances, however, a book not to be read casually! I've already mentioned Wittgenstein in note 3 to chapter 1, regarding his lectures on religion. But if you're truly interested in his thought, then *Philosophical Investigations* is the place to begin—provided you proceed with caution, patience, and some Advil ready at hand.
6. If I were to recommend one serious philosophical work on the question of God—a work that does purport to make original contributions—it would be J. L. Mackie's *The Miracle of Belief.* Mackie was an excellent philosopher who wrote an extremely important and still highly influential book on ethics. His book on God isn't quite as important or well known, but it presents strong, philosophically serious criticisms of a number of arguments for the existence of God. I should say that Mackie, unlike me, claims that we can indeed have a concept of God. But oddly enough he makes this particular claim very, very briefly and not very convincingly—or so I think—which is out of character with the rest of the book.
7. The playoff system being what it is, this is technically inaccurate. Instead of "pennant," I should say "division championship." But you get the idea. And if, by the way, I seem to be using more

than my share of sports analogies, I apologize. But they do come in handy. Sports turns out to be a massively important area of modern life and philosophers use sports analogies all the time.

3. THE IMPOSSIBLE DREAM

1. You could get picky and say that we don't rule out the possibility of Santa existing. Rather, what we rule out is the possibility of certain things happening that involve Santa—namely, all the things that Santa's supposed to do. That's okay. Either way is fine with me, at least for present purposes.
2. Of course, the difference between discovering something new about the world and changing the world isn't especially clear. Sometimes we change the world only because we've made new discoveries. Sometimes we discover something new only because of changes we've made. Today we can fly, something we couldn't do before. Is this because we've discovered something new about the world—principles of aerodynamics—or because we built an airplane that worked and that needed to be explained? An important question—but not for present purposes. In either case, the world as we understand it and as we experience it is different from what we understood and experienced before.
3. Though if you analyzed these cases using formal logic—if you traced out very carefully the logic of what's actually being said—I suspect you'd find that they too are of the type that says of something that it's both X and non-X at the same time.

4. EVEN IF THE FLESH IS WILLING

1. Notice, by the way, that this is probably a version of the so-called mind-body problem. A tough problem indeed. Supposedly we all have minds and we all have bodies, and those two things—the mind and the body—interact in powerful ways so that we actu-

ally do things. This is sometimes called Cartesian dualism. But if the mind is immaterial and the body is matter, how could this kind of interaction actually take place? How can the immaterial mind (which is kind of like a physical vacuum) hit or move or otherwise touch and engage with a physical body (which is very much like a baseball)? Please don't expect me to answer this one! In fact, I wouldn't touch it with a ten-foot pole. (I should also say that the issue of weighing justice in ounces and pounds might be another version of the same problem, though it would take some philosophical work to show that.)

2. Hume was actually Scottish. And Berkeley was Irish. Samuel Clarke—now there was an Englishman.

5. ATHEISM . . .

1. It's true that some people who call themselves atheists deny that they deny the existence of God. Rather, they say that they simply lack a belief in God, which is certainly not the same thing. Now I suppose that such a position technically would qualify as "atheism"—without God—but I find it largely indistinguishable from agnosticism, especially since people who are atheistic in this way are so usually because of what they perceive as a lack of evidence. In any event, it's certainly the case that many atheists do actively say that God does not exist, and those are the people I'm calling atheists. As for the others, I think what I have to say about agnosticism would apply to them quite well.
2. What if the world doesn't exist? How do we know it does? Here—unlike the situation with the ontological argument (see note 2 to chapter 1)—I'd argue that we really can rely on good old Descartes. You'll recall that he's the one who said: "I think therefore I am." Now what exactly does that mean? Well, let's begin at the beginning. There's no question that I think. That

simply cannot be doubted. It's impossible for me, sitting here at my computer and kicking out text, not to believe that I am thinking. That's something I know. After all, for me to *deny* that I was thinking would require, could not happen without, the *thought* that I am not thinking; but the thought that I am not thinking would be, well, a thought; it couldn't be anything else but a thought; and I could only have that thought if I were—you guessed it—thinking. So the thought that I am not thinking is a thought that defeats itself. Ergo, I must be thinking.

Now it might be that all of the rest of my thoughts are false. Specifically, it might be that my body, my desk, my computer, my publisher, my readers—all of the stuff out there that I'm thinking about—maybe all of it's an illusion. Maybe I am not what I think I am—all arms and legs and hair and history—but really just a brain in a vat whose thoughts are being manipulated by an evil demon. In other words, maybe it's all just a dream. No desk, no computer, no arms, no hair. But even if that were true, I would still have to believe in the existence of the world. Maybe the world is, in fact, a lot smaller than I thought. Maybe it's really composed of only three things: one brain, one vat, and one demon. Nothing else. But the fact is that those things—the brain, the vat, and the demon—would exist; and if they existed, then so does the world. For as long as even only one thing exists, we have a world.

But then, of course, that puts us back to square one. For if one thing exists that constitutes the whole world, we're still required, under the logic of cause and effect, to ask where that thing came from. We have to believe that it came from somewhere. We have to believe (here we go again) that something created it, a First Thing. At which point we have to ask where that First Thing came from, and where did the creator of the (no longer) First

Thing come from, and so on ad infinitum. On this score, Descartes is of no help. But on the prior question of the existence of the world, he's actually pretty darn good.

3. "Meaning" is really a tough one. When a dog barks or a floor creaks or thunder claps, those are mere noises that, like ghroblingat, have no meaning. But you might say, wait a minute: a barking dog "means" it's hungry or angry or happy; a creaking floor "means" somebody's walking around; a clap of thunder "means" rain is on its way. And so, noises like that really do have meaning. That's what you might say. Well, as a math professor once commented on one of my answers: "Yes. But then again, no."

   If you want to pursue the general question of meaning, check out a great essay by H. P. Grice entitled—what else?—"Meaning." Grossly oversimplified, Grice says that the word "meaning," in English, really has two quite different meanings. He calls the first one "natural meaning." That's what the word *means* means when we say that the thunderclap means rain. It refers to a natural, physical process of cause and effect; and so too with the barking dog and the creaking floor. But then there's also "non-natural meaning." That's what the word *means* means when you're talking about a human being who is intentionally using language to get another human being to understand an idea or concept. The thunderclap isn't intending to use language to communicate an idea. Thunderclaps can't do that. But we can do that; and we do it all the time. In fact that's what I'm doing right now, this instant. I'm intentionally using language to communicate to you some set of concepts.

   This, by the way, also helps explain why animals—including chimps and whales and dolphins—really can't use language, even if it sometimes seems they do. But don't get me started . . .

7. FULL FAITH AND NO CREDIT

1. Emphasize "largely." Paul's letters—they are examples of the genre that scholars call the "diatribe"—are complex literary and philosophical documents, and we need to be careful about reading them too simplistically. So for example, his first letter to the Corinthians does talk about "knowledge" and the "power to interpret" as well as faith, and his letter to the Romans mentions the "law" that is "written in [our] hearts." Nonetheless, and in the last analysis, I think Paul believes deep down that pure faith is way more important than all this other stuff. It's the heart and soul of Christianity. In lots of ways, Paul's a very anti-intellectual guy—though for some of his defenders those will be fighting words.
2. Of course, there's another question. If you believe in Jesus, what does that actually mean? What part of Jesus are you believing in? Is it his existence, or his divinity, or his teachings, or his story, or his deeds? Those are not the same thing. So here, in part, is where interpreters of Paul strongly disagree with one another. But all of that is a matter of theology and, like I say, I'm no theologian.

8. IT'S ALL IN A GOOD CAUSE

1. Of course, what's true of science in general is, in this respect, also true of so-called intelligent design theology. The intelligent design argument, like the cosmological argument and the ontological argument, purports to be an argument for the existence of God. However, it seems to me—and to tons of other people—that it presupposes, but doesn't explain, the origin of the universe. It leaves the basic question unaddressed. It doesn't explain—and generally doesn't try to explain—how there can be something that absolutely must exist and cannot possibly exist at

the same time. I think this is actually true of lots of theologies—for example, things that are called "process" theology and "liberation" theology. You should perhaps know that there are really lots of interesting theories for helping us understand why it might be that God does this or that, or why God allows this or that to happen, and so on. But those are also theories that come into play only *after* we accept the existence of God. They are theories for theists, but they're not theories that justify theism. (And of course, that's a pretty serious problem, since they're talking about an idea—the idea of God—that's really not an idea at all.)

2. In the spirit of there's nothing new under the sun, you should know that Plato, in a work called the *Timaeus*, seems to have anticipated some of these ideas, especially the notion that before the world was created there was no time. But for more on Plato, see chapter 10.
3. It's worth noting that Dostoevsky, that rascal, had guys like me pegged a long time ago. As Ivan Karamazov explains to his brother:

> If God exists and if he indeed created the earth, then, as we know perfectly well, he created it in accordance with Euclidean geometry, and he created human reason with a conception of only three dimensions of space. At the same time there were and are even now geometers and philosophers, even some of the most outstanding of them, who doubt that the whole universe, or, even more broadly, the whole of being, was created purely in accordance with Euclidean geometry; they even dare to dream that two parallel lines, which according to Euclid cannot possibly meet on earth, may perhaps meet somewhere in infinity. I, my dear, have come to the

> conclusion that if I cannot understand even that, then it is not for me to understand about God. I humbly confess that I do not have any ability to resolve such questions. I have a Euclidean mind, an earthly mind, and therefore it is not for us to resolve things that are not of this world. And I advise you never to think about it, Alyosha my friend, and most especially about whether God exists or not. All such questions are completely unsuitable to a mind created with a concept of only three dimensions. (Translation by Richard Pevear and Larissa Volokhonsky [1990])

If that isn't cool, I don't know what is. I would add that, as far as I can tell, Ivan—or Fyodor—didn't talk about Conceptual Impossibility, so he wasn't exactly aproleptic. But he was pretty clearly moving in that direction. You should also know that Dostoevsky wrote this particular passage in 1878 or 1879, hence about the exact time that Einstein himself was floating around in his mommy's womb.

4. What's the big deal about 480 BCE? That's when the Greeks, led by Athens, finally defeated the Persians, who had invaded Greece ten years earlier. Among other things, this solidified the position of Athens as the most important of the Greek city-states. But then there was Sparta. That, however, is another story.
5. Though I shouldn't oversimplify too much. The Greeks certainly did know about, and were very worried about, the role of luck or chance in the universe. Indeed, if they weren't worried about luck, they probably wouldn't have needed to invent gods to help impose some sense of order on things.
6. Here I follow, and steal from, a wonderful and important article that I highly recommend, "Freedom and Resentment" by P. F.

Strawson—who happens to be, for what it's worth, just about my favorite philosopher of the twentieth century. Of course, favorite probably means I agree with him a lot.

7. Am I saying that the human brain is hardwired to think about the world in terms of cause and effect? Well, I'm not, but I might. I'm actually making an observation. Thinking about the world in terms of cause and effect is—I observe—what all ordinary people do; it's an essential part of what it means to make sense, at least according to our lights. Now exactly why is this so? I don't know. What caused it? (No pun intended, because it's really not a pun.) I have no idea. But I must say that the universality of the logic of cause and effect does make something like the hardwiring hypothesis attractive.

   Such a hypothesis has its roots, I'd argue, in the philosophy of Kant (see note 2 to chapter 1), who claimed, as I'm claiming, that human thought necessarily involves notions of cause and effect (though he said it necessarily involves much, much else besides—a claim that I don't dispute) and that this is somehow a constitutive feature of what it means to be a rational creature. Kant, like me, doesn't say that the world really is a matter of cause and effect. Kant, like me, is agnostic on that question. Rather, he says that *if* we're having thoughts and experiences about the world, then those thoughts and experiences must operate under the logic of cause and effect. He also says that we cannot deny that we're having thoughts and experiences about the world, though we might be wrong. So we have no choice but to think about things in terms of cause and effect, even though all of this might be a total delusion—a delusion that we could never possibly discover.

   As a Kantian, I myself like all of that a lot. It's not exactly a hardwiring hypothesis, but it tends in that direction. So, for example, there are those who believe that all human languages share certain deep structural similarities, despite their obvious differences, and that those similarities reflect a certain universal, hardwired capacity in the human brain not just for language but for language having those deep structural properties. Others have argued that our ability to create and listen to music reflects innate, hardwired distinctions between, say, consonance and dissonance—as reflected, arguably, in the physics of the overtone system—and that this explains why some music sounds good and some doesn't, even accepting the great variety of musical styles and musical tastes. I'm attracted to all this, but I'm certainly not prepared to defend it. Not only am I not a theologian or an anthropologist; I'm also neither a linguist nor a musicologist nor a psychologist of language acquisition or of musical perception. I'm just trying to reconstruct—and make sense of—our ordinary way of thinking about things.

But you should also know that a number of psychologists—cognitive scientists—have in fact directly studied such questions, and that the evidence, as I understand it, powerfully supports the claim that the logic of cause and effect is universal. There seems to be overwhelming agreement among developmental psychologists that babies around the age of six months begin to think in terms of cause and effect. Exactly why this is the case—and exactly how causal thinking grows and matures—is a matter of dispute. But the basic claim seems not to be in doubt; and it's hard to imagine how tiny little babies could think in terms of cause and effect unless this was, in some sense, a natural, inherent, inborn feature of the human mind.

9. DETECTIVE FICTION

1. Notice that the reverse is not true. Not everything to be solved is a mystery. Equations and crossword puzzles, for example.

2. Of course, not all of Sherlock Holmes's mysteries were murder mysteries. But you get the idea.

10. AN INKLING OF . . .

1. It's conventional and probably correct to say that serious and systematic thought in the West began with a guy named Thales, around 600 BCE, or a little more than two hundred years before Plato. In the scheme of things, this makes Plato very, very early indeed.
2. So in Hesiod, Cronos the son castrates Ouranos the father. Here, Euthyphro is seriously considering bringing criminal charges against his old man. Of course, at around the same time, Sophocles is writing a complex story—pun intended—about a son named Oedipus who murders a father named Laius. Do you see a pattern here? And read on. When we get to Plato, the pattern will continue—though not so violently.
3. The idea that piety is, in some important way, a matter of respect for dad—"filial piety"—is pretty common in Western literature. Perhaps the locus classicus is Virgil's *Aeneid.* The hero, Aeneas, is constantly referred to as pious, but his piety seems to be directed above all to his father, Anchises. How this plays out in light of the history, in the ancient world, of sons killing—or castrating—fathers is an interesting question.
4. Though we do need to be a little bit careful about this. It's true: Athens was a democracy. Decisions were made by a vote of the citizens. But it's also true that a pretty large chunk of the Athenian population was composed of slaves, and slaves could not vote. And it's true as well that another very large chunk of the Athenian population was composed of "metics" or resident aliens who came from elsewhere and who lived in Athens; Metics also could not vote. Of course, about half the population of Athens

was female, and women couldn't vote either. So Athenian democracy was a democracy of the relatively few. But a democracy nonetheless.

5. You should know, if you don't already, that Plato, in addition to being a philosopher, was a great literary artist. As I've already said, the conversation between Euthyphro and Socrates was written up by Plato in a work called "Euthyphro." But the phrase "written up" is misleading. Consider, for example, the simple fact that the conversation in question was a private one. Euthyphro and Socrates were talking to each other and, at least according to Plato's own report, no one else was there. Just the two of them. So how does Plato know exactly what was said? Now certainly either Euthyphro or Socrates could have told Plato afterwards what was said. But that couldn't have been anything other than a more or less rough report, and certainly not a word-for-word recitation. Plato had no transcript, no tape recording, no exact record of Euthyphro's and Socrates's words. At the very least, then, he's inventing their actual words. He's making it up. He's writing dialogue.

   Of course, it's also possible that the discussion between Euthyphro and Socrates never really took place at all, and that Plato invented not just their words but the whole event. No reason to believe otherwise. But even if that's true, it doesn't necessarily mean that Plato's report is entirely false. It certainly could be, and in fact probably was, an accurate reflection of Socrates's actual thoughts about piety. In any case, it's clear that Plato is not just a transcriber but an author who is making a lot of literary decisions. And it seems likely that one such decision was to tell the world—whether accurately or not—that Socrates, while on his way to a trial to defend himself against a charge of heterodoxy or atheism, had a discussion about piety, religion, and the gods.

Let me put it another way: the fact that Socrates had such a discussion on such a topic immediately prior to his trial is either a remarkable coincidence or, more likely, a reflection of the literary sensibilities of Plato.

6. Though actually there'd be plenty of competition, including fellows named Solon, Peisistratus, Cleisthenes, Ephialtes, and a few others. Lots of political talent in ancient Athens.
7. Well sure, we could feel things. Sightless people feel things and make distinctions all the time, important distinctions. But don't be too tough on Plato—or on me. After all, it's just a metaphor.

11. . . . THE TRUTH

1. By the way, from this you shouldn't conclude that morality goes out the window. The notion that morality requires God—that without God there is no foundation for right and wrong—is simply absurd. Many of the great moral systems do not presuppose the existence of God; and surely some of the purest souls who ever lived did not believe in God.

   Now others will argue that that's all well and good, but for morality to be truly effective—for most people actually to behave in moral ways—there has to be religion. Even if religion is based on an impossibility—even if religion is based on a concept of God that in fact is not a concept at all—it's still an enormously useful thing. Religion has *utility*. It helps prevent people from savaging one another. It's a bulwark of ethical behavior, of civility, of peace, of justice. If sometimes religion screws things up, just think how much worse things would be without it.

   I need to say two things about this. First, the problem of religion is completely and entirely different from the problem I'm addressing in this book. The problem I'm addressing in this book is the problem of God, and that's a problem about our conceptual apparatus, about what concepts we actually have and can have. The question of the usefulness—the utility—of religion is totally different. That's a question about what works and what doesn't work in society—a sociological or historical or political question, not a conceptual one. There's really very little connection between the two issues. Second, however, I can't help but say that the claim that religion is a necessary (much less necessary *and* sufficient) condition for morality really does strike me as silly. Consider, if nothing else, this simple test: is it really the case that all nonreligious people are immoral and is it really the case that all religious people are moral? Nobody could possibly believe either statement. Consider another, perhaps more reasonable test: are religious people *generally* more moral than nonreligious people? You might think so, but that's not been my experience, and it'd be awfully difficult to prove. Consider, then, a third, even better test: is it really the case, as a historical matter, that deeply religious societies tend to behave better than secular ones? It would be a strange historian indeed who would say that.

Now I won't pursue the issue in any detail because, again, this book is not about religion. Nonetheless, and just for the record, I myself am not a big fan. I don't like religion one bit. Indeed, I dislike it intensely.

Of course, there's no doubt that tons and tons of good people have done tons and tons of good things in the name of religion. But the claim that they have done them *because* of religion—now that's an entirely different matter. Would good people suddenly stop doing good things if religion ceased to exist? Not the ones I know.

The situation, however, is actually more complicated than this. On the one hand, and as a historical matter, the record of religion isn't great. In fact, I actually think it's pretty horrific overall. And yet, you also have to remember that a knockdown argument against religion isn't nearly enough to show that avowedly atheistic societies are any better. Does, for example, the name Joe Stalin ring a bell? The Brotherhood of Human Brutality is, history seems to suggest, an equal opportunity employer.

2. I am unaware of any work of literature that evokes the willies more profoundly than the great play by Tom Stoppard, *Rosencrantz and Guildenstern Are Dead.* If you haven't seen it, go. Of course, Shakespeare's *Hamlet*—the inspiration for Stoppard's play—doesn't do such a bad job of it itself.
3. Here, perhaps, is one way in which my argument is different from something called "negative theology." Roughly speaking, negative theology is the view that we can't say anything at all about what God is like, other than that God exists, but that we *can* say lots of things about what God plainly isn't. For example, I am plainly not God, so God must be fundamentally unlike me. Such a view has sometimes been attributed to an important thinker of late antiquity called the Pseudo-Dionysius. I myself have some doubts about that, though again I'm no theologian. But in any event, my problem with this general approach should now be obvious: for the life of me I can't see how one can say anything at all about God, positive or negative, without getting caught up in hopeless conceptual nonsense.
4. Nope. No women on the list. Which reflects, I'd say, some very ugly facts of history. But there's hope. I do political philosophy for a living, and in my opinion the most brilliant and most important political philosopher of the twentieth century, the one who'll be studied more than any other in centuries to come, was a woman—Hannah Arendt. Of course, there are also no non-Westerners on the list. Which reflects, I'd say, some very ugly

facts about my own education. But I know enough to know that one would have no trouble constructing an equally impressive list of writers and artists and scientists who lived and worked in, for example, East Asia, South Asia, and the lands once governed by the Caliphate.

ACKNOWLEDGMENTS

I owe a large debt of gratitude to Steve Wasserstrom, who read an early version of this book and offered comments and suggestions that proved to be, at once, extremely reassuring and enormously helpful. His enthusiasm and insight were, and are, deeply appreciated. Pete Rock also read an early version, and his reactions—especially regarding, shall we say, literary matters—were most encouraging. The reactions of Jim Rutman to the same materials were the opposite of encouraging, but he did provide an important and useful bit of practical advice for which I am appreciative. In a rather different vein, I benefited from Wally Engert's typically excellent philological expertise, while David Griffiths was wonderfully helpful in softening some of the sharp edges of my own mathematical and scientific ignorance.

I am also very grateful to Columbia University Press in general and to Senior Executive Editor Wendy Lochner in particular, for being willing to pursue a project that is, perhaps, somewhat outside of their usual comfort zone, and for doing so with top-of-the-line professionalism.

A heartfelt thanks, as well, to all of the friends, neighbors, acquaintances, colleagues, tutors, merchants, purveyors, fellow travelers, and assorted comrades-in-arms who operate in and around the area between Montparnasse and Invalides, along with its various tributaries from Rennes to Gobelins, and who—with respect to art, grammar, travel, squash (the game, not the gourd), pastry (along with butter, bread, cheese, veal, and related food items far too numerous to mention), conversation, gossip, scholarly exchange, intellectual engagement, and warm companionship, among many other things—provided the kind of moral sustenance that makes life worth living and that makes writing a book seem like a natural part of *la vie quotidienne*.

Closer to home, Tom Steinberger made a number of excellent recommendations that have been incorporated into the book, much to its advantage. Tom, moreover, is only one of three children, Catherine and Julia being the other two, who had to listen to my arguments over a great many years and in a great many venues—at the dinner table, in the car, on the practice field, and so on—and whose endurance, tolerance, skepticism, and overall brainpower were instrumental in helping me put my thoughts into some kind of orderly form. Each of them also knows quite well that my very best critic is their mother—which is merely one of the reasons, though far from the most important, that it was for her that this book, like all of my books, was written.

Finally, and as always, I am deeply indebted to Reed College—a community of endlessly stimulating colleagues and astonishingly good students that honors, above all, the life of the mind and that sustains, more than any place of which I'm aware, the activity of being an intellectual.

INDEX OF NAMES